SHOREHAM AIRPORT

AN ILLUSTRATED HISTORY

PETER C. BROWN

First published 2014

Amberley Publishing
The Hill, Stroud
Gloucestershire, GL5 4EP

www.amberley-books.com

British Library Cataloguing in Publication Data.
A catalogue record for this book is available from the British Library.

ISBN 978 1 4456 3344 2 (print)
ISBN 978 1 4456 3355 8 (ebook)

Typeset in 10.5pt on 14pt Sabon.
Typesetting and Origination by Amberley Publishing.
Printed in the UK.

Contents

Introduction   5

1   Those Magnificent Men   7

2   1914–1918 The First World War   15

3   1919–1939 Between the Wars   19

4   1940–1945 The Second World War   26

5   1946–1959 Post-War and Recovery   39

6   1960–1969 The Beagle Has Landed   56

7   1970–1989 The Way Ahead Part I   70

8   1985–2005 The Way Ahead Part II   77

9   2006–2014 All Change   106

10   Shoreham Airport Rescue and Firefighting Service (SARFFS)   128

Photographs of Shoreham   136

Bibliography   160

Introduction

Shoreham (Brighton City) Airport (EGKA) is the oldest licensed airport in the UK (established in 1910), and was used as a military airfield in both world wars. Situated in 200 acres west of Shoreham-by-Sea, at Lancing in the Adur district of West Sussex, it is immediately to the south of the A27 between Brighton and Worthing. It has its own railway station on the West Coastway railway line, and can be reached within a few minutes from Brighton, Hove, or Worthing. It also adjoins Shoreham-by-Sea harbour, one of the staging grounds for the preparations for D-Day, 6 June 1944.

Its beautiful Grade II listed art deco terminal building was built in 1936 and has been a popular location for film-makers seeking to portray scenes of the 1930s for television programmes such as *Tenko*, *Poirot*, *Fortunes of War*, and more recently the film *The Da Vinci Code*. It is still in everyday use by business, training and pleasure fliers alike, including many visitors from Europe. A unique war memorial stands near the entrance to Shoreham airport: a marble plaque providing a dedication to the British, Commonwealth and Allied servicemen and -women who gave their lives in the First and Second World Wars. The plaque sits below a propeller recovered from a United States Air Force B-26C Martin Marauder medium bomber that came down in the English Channel in June 1944.

In the days of early aviation, flying machines were made of wood, canvas and wire, and were usually propelled by underpowered engines. If the wind was not too strong, they could leave the ground at under 40 mph with a top speed of about 50 mph, so there was a 10 mph margin. Flying above that speed often resulted in the engine overheating, or the stresses causing the wires or wood within the aircraft to snap; flying below that speed caused the machine to stall or spin.

Shoreham was the aerodrome for several aviation pioneers, including Oscar Morison and Grahame Gilmour, and was the base where the Pashley and Miles brothers set up their respective businesses. The airfield soon became established as a major flying centre, with air shows featuring aircraft 'looping the loop', attempting to break altitude records and dropping bombs, illuminated night flying, and both long- and short-distance record-breaking air races that involved pilots from all over Europe.

The airport had only grass landing strips until a hard runway was opened in 1982, heralding an immediate and permanent increase in flying movements, and since 1989 it has been the venue for the RAFA annual air show, which has grown into one of the UK's finest air shows, with a fantastic air display which attracts over 40,000 people each year to watch aircraft from all periods of aviation history.

CHAPTER 1
Those Magnificent Men

The town of Shoreham-by-Sea is an ancient seaport built on a south-facing slope situated between the South Downs and the English Channel. Bordered by the A27 to the north, the River Adur to the west, the town of Southwick to the east, and the railway line to Brighton to the south, the aerodrome was built on the western side of the river, on an area that was formerly a salt marsh, about 6 miles west of Brighton and 5 miles east of Worthing.

Cecil Pashley 'catching the train'. (J&C McCutcheon Collection)

In October 1909, negotiations began between Edward Geere, Captain Alexander Bruce Siddons Fraser and James Gurney Denton, the mayors of Brighton, Hove and Worthing respectively, and George Arthur Wingfield's Aviators Finance Co., over a proposal to build a permanent aerodrome for expert and student aviators alike, of all nations. They realised its position was attractive to sightseers, and would provide easy access to London and the Continent; the new industry would also create many jobs for local people. Wingfield, a Brighton solicitor, had already leased some 200 acres of land at New Salts Farm between Bungalow Town (which was constructed on the shingle spit extending between Lancing and Shoreham) and Lancing College, comprising what is now the south-east corner of the present Shoreham airfield.

In the early months of 1910, the London-based artist Harold Hume 'Piff' Piffard, who was associated with the Aviators Finance Co. Ltd, set himself up on a piece of grazing land across the river from Shoreham. A former scholar at the Lancing College, he was a fine painter of military and costume subjects, and had exhibited four works at the Royal Academy, two works at the Royal Society of Artists in Birmingham, and several works at Liverpool. He also had a keen interest in designing and constructing model aeroplanes, and by May 1910, he had built a box kite 'pusher' biplane (which was based on the French Farman III) in a shed (they were not called hangars at the time) that was constructed in the south-east corner of the field, close to the railway bridge.

The experimental flying machine, which he named *Hummingbird*, was powered by a 40-hp engine, which drove a 7-foot-diameter pusher propeller mounted at the rear of the pilot, yet Piffard only managed a series of hops before managing to stay airborne long enough to qualify as his first flight on 10 July. Unfortunately, a collision with a shed on his second landing badly damaged his aircraft, but undaunted, he set about making repairs. Alfred Evans, the landlord of the Sussex Pad Inn opposite the airfield on the Old Shoreham Road, had been watching the flying experiments with interest, and offered Piffard the challenge that if he could fly his machine over to collect it, he would give him a crate of champagne.

Piffard flew *Hummingbird* over the ¾-mile distance 30–40 feet above the ground in forty seconds, and won the challenge. The flight was more complicated for Piffard because it included a turn, which until then he had not been able to achieve.

The aeroplane was damaged beyond repair in another crash in October, and Piffard set about designing and building another aircraft in a temporary shed on the beach at Bungalow Town. The aircraft, which he called *Hummingbird II*, was a floatplane, but on its first trial it capsized. Further trials were unsuccessful, and Piffard, who by now had run out of money, abandoned flying altogether and resumed his career as an artist. He had only been at Shoreham for a few months, but his place in aviation history, as the first man to build and fly a powered aeroplane over Sussex, was assured. A memorial garden was laid out to celebrate his first flight, and it is also commemorated by the café/bar in the airport terminal being named after the aeroplane.

Negotiations had taken place between George Wingfield and the London, Brighton & South Coast Railway for a new station to serve the aerodrome. The line provided excellent links for the South Coast and London, and would become a popular destination for the large crowds that attended the pioneering 'air shows'. A wooden platform called *Bungalow Town Halt* (situated where New Salts Farm Road now meets the airport perimeter road) was opened on 1 October 1910, and by the end of the year, other aviators had started to arrive to experiment and test their flying machines, and despite the site being prone to flooding, the flying ground was established.

On 7 March 1911, Oscar Colin Morison (who had gained his Royal Aero Club aviator's certificate on 31 December 1910, and had flown exhibition flights in the early days of aviation in England) became the first aviator to fly in to Shoreham, arriving in his Blériot monoplane from Brighton, and on 6 May, after it had been postponed three times because of bad weather, the first Brooklands–Shoreham Air Race was held (Shoreham was nominated as the turning point), providing clear evidence of the progress that was being made in aviation.

Harold Piffard and his Type-D Hydro biplane in 1911. (Author's Collection)

Four aircraft competed in this well-advertised handicap race, the first point-to-point race of its kind in the UK: Gustav Hamel on his Blériot monoplane, Douglas Graham Gilmour on a Bristol Type 'T' biplane, Lieutenant Snowden-Smith on a British-built Henri Farman biplane which was constructed by Hewlett and Blondeau, and Howard Pixton on an Avro biplane. As soon as the aviators were in the air, a large crowd began to collect along the seafront at Brighton to watch the exciting spectacle.

Hamel was the clear leader, and circled around the captive balloon on the Palace Pier before descending to make an easy landing at Shoreham. The next to arrive was Snowden-Smith, but he had to forfeit the second prize. His method of having his map sewn round his left trouser leg above the knee for reference was primitive and, not knowing the area, he misread it and steered a course that took him a mile inside the perimeter of the course before aiming for Brighton Pier and then Shoreham. There was no alternative but to disqualify him. Gilmore was the third to arrive, and Pixton landed some time later, having decided to land at the first suitable place he found to ask for directions after he lost his bearings.

Hamel won the race in fifty-seven minutes and ten seconds, but, after a break of only twenty minutes, he returned to Brooklands, where he arrived just thirty-four minutes later, breaking the record he had just set. The prize money was awarded to the aviators on the following Monday by the mayoress, Mrs Thomas Stanford; the £80 winning prize went to Hamel, £30 each to the second and third places, and £20 to Snowden-Smith.

The big-prize races continued throughout the year, including the Calais–Hendon race, which started on 29 May, in which Frank Barra, Roland Garros, Eugène Gilbert, Albert 'Beaumont' Kimmerling, Eugène Renaux, Maurice Tabuteau, M Emile Train, Jules Védrines, and James Valentine (the only British entry) took part.

Shoreham aerodrome was officially opened on 20 June 1911 by the mayors of Brighton, Hove, and Worthing. A spectator's grandstand had been built for the 'Circuit of Europe' and 'Round Britain' races, and six wooden sheds had been constructed.

The aerodrome became the starting point for the earliest recorded commercial cargo flight when Horatio Barber took a consignment of Osram light bulbs for the General Electric Company to Wish Park in Hove in his Valkyrie monoplane on 4 July.

On 22 July, the *Daily Mail* 'Race around Britain' started from Brooklands. A circuit of 1,010 miles had been designed, and included thirteen compulsory stops and checkpoints (Shoreham being one of these), to push the early aviators and their machines to their limits. The £10,000 prize money was collected by Lieutenant de Vaisseau Conneau (flying as André Beaumont); James Valentine was again the only English competitor, and completed the five-day-long circuit, finishing in third place.

The Shoreham Flying Club was founded by Cecil Lawrence 'Pash' Pashley and his brother Eric Clowes in the autumn of 1911, both of whom taught themselves to fly two years earlier (and only gained their brevets during this year), and in November 1911, the Chanter Flying School relocated to Shoreham from Hendon, and occupied two of the newly built sheds with their two Anzani-Blériot flying machines. Piffard's old shed had been converted into the aerodrome restaurant.

Alliott Verdon Roe, who had founded Avro on 1 January 1910, was among other pioneering aviators such as Claude Grahame-White, Gordon England, Horatio Barber, Douglas Graham Gilmour, John Alcock, and Tsoe K. Wong (one of the earliest Chinese aviators) who arrived to use the aerodrome in 1912 (Avro rented shed number four). Aviation experimenters such as George Miller Dyott, with his red mid-wing monoplane, and Cedric Lee and Tilghman Richards, with their annular monoplane, which was referred to as the 'flying doughnut', also arrived.

A fire broke out on 29 February which destroyed three sheds, and despite the best efforts by flying club members to rescue some of the aeroplanes, it was the beginning of the end for the Chanter Flying School. Compounding the misfortune that had fallen upon the aerodrome at this time, the owners also lost a court case relating to unpaid fees associated with the cargo flight made by Horatio Barber in the previous July.

The pioneer British aviator Gustav Hamel. (Author's Collection)

The Aviators Finance Co. Ltd changed its name to the Brighton-Shoreham Aerodrome Ltd, of which George Wingfield was the chairman; its principal object was the development of aviation in the UK. James Radley also arrived at Shoreham during the year to set up his engineering works, where he made modifications to a Blériot XI racing monoplane for William Barnard Rhodes-Moorhouse (who as a Lieutenant would go on to become the winner of the RFC's first Victoria Cross).

By the end of 1912 there were two military and sixteen civilian flying schools in operation, including Avro, whose CFI was Herbert Rutter Simms (who had been apprenticed by A. V. Roe at Manchester), and used their Avro Type-D, and later their prototype Type-E and Avro 500, aircraft for tuition. They were also well established as builders of aeroplanes for private customers, with a dozen orders in hand.

The years of endeavour were starting to pay off for Alliott Roe, who re-formed his business as a limited company on 11 January 1913, and had also been given the honour of escorting HM King George V at the Olympia Aero Show, held between 14–22 February. His company was moved to larger premises in Manchester in April to meet the demand of aeroplane production for the War Office.

Captain Beatty of the Royal Flying Corps (RFC) visited Shoreham, where he met with a representative of the owners of the aerodrome to inspect the landing ground and sheds for its suitability for operations by an RFC squadron. Against

Harold Piffard's Hydro-plane. (Author's Collection)

the backdrop of these preparations, a series of weekly meetings took place to give flyers and aviation experimenters the opportunity to show off their skills in the air, and despite a relatively small number of machines being available, many good exhibitions were given. On 18 May, Avro pilot Frederick Raynham flew the first Avro 503 floatplane from the River Adur, and over the following days of testing, the aircraft proved to be a success. The Avro 504 was subsequently fitted with floats and tested soon afterwards.

Eric Pashley would thrill the inhabitants of Bungalow Town and the spectators in the grandstand with spirals and high-banked turns. Sadly, Shoreham airport's first fatality occurred on 29 June 1913, when Richard Norton Wright stalled his Avro 500 and crashed in the garden of New Salts Farm.

Flying restrictions had been put in place by July, and the Home Secretary, Mr Reginald McKenna, explained that it was in the interests of national safety that foreign flyers would require special exemption to fly over prohibited areas of the Thames, as described by the War Office. It was vehemently argued that this had a detrimental impact on the aerial practice which was necessary for adequate training, but nevertheless, pleasure flying and flying instruction did continue.

The Radley-England Waterplane was a four-bay biplane designed and built in secrecy in shed number six by James Radley and Gordon England, and powered by three 50-hp Gnome engines which were uniquely mounted in series. It made its debut flight for testing its readiness for the £10,000 Circuit of Britain race in August, but the pilot, Gordon England, struck a marker buoy with one of the floats, which filled with water, and the aircraft sank.

The Avro Flying School left Shoreham in September. The once viable business had been marred by complaints from customers about the poor condition of their aircraft, and even their chief pilot had left a few months earlier following a dispute over their Bruga monoplane.

The Lee-Richards annular monoplane had taken months to build and test, which was done in great secrecy. It made its first flight on 23 November 1913, but a design flaw of being tail-heavy caused the aircraft to stall and crash; the pilot, Gordon England, sustained injury to his knee, and it grounded him for several weeks. The aircraft was rebuilt and the 'Mark II' proved to be more stable, but further testing was curtailed as the war clouds were gathering over Europe. Following this, Cedric Lee decided to rebuild and modify his prototype to enter it in the Gordon Bennett Air Race held in Paris in September 1914, but with war on the horizon, the project was curtailed.

The Pashley Brothers with their Farman biplane outside the hangars at Shoreham airport in 1912. (Author's Collection)

Two De Havilland DH60G Gypsy Moths (G-AADA and G-ABTS) in front of a crowded apron. (Clive Barker)

CHAPTER 2

1914–1918
The First World War

The management of Shoreham aerodrome implemented a number of improvements in the arrangements at the ground, which made the weekly flying meetings very popular. The ground, being absolutely level, was fit for purpose, and the racing course was marked off by pylons which kept the competitors fairly close to the enclosures so that an excellent view of how the different pilots handled their machines could be obtained.

Several new sheds had been erected to accommodate visitors' machines, and alongside these was the headquarters for the Sussex County Aero Club. There were other attractions, such as a tennis court and tea gardens, together with a military band on race days, that provided a very good programme of music. Captain C. A. Tyrer, the aerodrome manager, and his staff were rewarded for their efforts by the large crowds that the venue drew from all over the country by road or rail.

Cecil and Eric Pashley designed and built a small pusher biplane for competition flying, and the machine won its first race only a few days after it was completed, the occasion being the pylon race for the Shell Cup at the opening of the 1914 season. The tests of the new biplane were quite satisfactory, and it won the Brighton Cup in July as well as the speed race on the following day. Pashley piloted the machine above the clouds, and at times was completely lost to view.

Work had just started on a faster machine of the same type when war broke out on 4 August, and the aerodrome was requisitioned by the War Office. Pashley's flying school continued to operate until December, and their machines were put into storage in one of the sheds when they left; Cecil went to the Northern Lakes (and later to Hendon, where he underwent training for the RFC), and Eric went to Vickers as a test pilot before joining 24 Squadron in France (where he was killed in an accident while on active service).

From the beginning of the occupation of the aerodrome by the military, George Wingfield had instigated a costly action against the Government, although this didn't end until 1916, when he received £25,765 in compensation from them.

Shoreham became the home of the 24th Division, or 'K3' as it was known, which was part of Lord Kitchener's Third Army (he was Secretary of War when Britain declared war on Germany on 4 August). The area was selected because it had a railhead, seaport and airport in a strategic position on the South Coast. Very soon after, men started to arrive by rail, and local territorial soldiers began creating a tented camp on the Oxen Field, to the north of Mill Lane. They arrived in such numbers that many of the townsfolk were asked to assist by providing temporary housing and food for them. Buckingham Park was also being used as a tented Army camp, with a field kitchen and latrines dug to provide a modicum of hygiene. The situation was improved in early 1915 when accommodation huts, which were rapidly constructed during the winter of 1914/15, were deemed fit for habitation.

Major Eugene Louis Gerrard, RMLI (Royal Marines Light Infantry), who commanded No. 1 Squadron of the Royal Naval Air Service (which, while stationed in Antwerp and Dunkirk, carried out the first air raids on enemy targets), was in command of the aerodrome and all its assets, and immediately began recruiting pilots for the RFC. No. 3 Reserve Aeroplane Squadron were the first to arrive with their Farman 'Longhorn' pusher biplanes and Royal Aircraft Factory FE2s (they later included Avro 504s). The young men who passed through their six-week training programme, which initially included ten to twelve hours' flying time (this was dramatically reduced as the demand for more pilots grew) and a short gunnery course, were then sent to the Western Front to engage in aerial combat. The life expectancy of the young pilots was just eleven days, but many didn't survive more than three or four. Shoreham was the departure point for the very first flight of Blériots and Royal Aircraft Factory BEs to join the conflict across the Channel.

Pleasure and competition flying continued despite the occupation of the larger part of the aerodrome by the military. For short-distance races, the airfield course was a little over 1¾ miles long, marked out by pylons. The last pylon before the home straight was positioned so that competing aircraft had to bank steeply near the enclosures to provide spectators with an advantageous view of the pilots at their controls.

The air show of Saturday 11 July 1914 featured J. L. Hall in his Avro 502 biplane, Eric Pashley flying the Pashley brothers' own aircraft they had designed and built, Cecil Pashley flying an old Henry Farman biplane, Jack Alcock flying a Maurice Farman (Alcock was later to become famous, with Arthur Whitten-Brown, for crossing the Atlantic in a Vickers Vimy), and W. H. Elliott and G. J. Lusted, both in the older Henry Farman biplanes. For the races, there were a number of heats, and competitors were handicapped, starting in staggered fashion with the older, slower planes having a three-minute start on the fastest (Hall's Avro 502). Eric Pashley, Hall and Alcock qualified for the final, which Eric won convincingly by one minute and three seconds, and with it the cup and £70 prize money.

A 'Blériot Day' took place on Saturday 25 July, and included a speed race for a trophy and cash prize, and a bomb-dropping contest, but the Brighton Cup Race was cancelled due to the war. Elimination trials were still carried out in August ready for the Gordon Bennett Aviation Race to be held in France in the following year; Cedric Lee was the contestant from Shoreham. The trials took place at Upavon, and involved a slow-speed test and a speed test. The entrants had to fly in a straight line out and back – a distance of about 1½ miles – without touching the ground, and at a constant height of not more than one hundred feet. The speed test which followed had to be carried out around a 5-mile circuit, but with speeds not exceeding 45 mph, for a total distance of 125 miles.

The massive expansion of the British Army by the end of 1914 was reflected in an expansion of the RFC, and at Shoreham, this led to No. 14 Squadron being formed by Captain Alexander Ross-Hume from a nucleus from No. 3 Reserve Squadron on 3 February 1915, and placed under the command of Major George Todd. The unit started working up towards combat readiness with an assortment of aircraft, and moved firstly to Hounslow Heath, and then to Gosport where, along with 17 Squadron, it came under the operational control of 5 Wing RFC and worked upon a variety of aircraft types before departing for the Middle East in November.

Later in the year, the South East Area Flying Instructors School was established to evaluate some of the captured enemy aircraft that were stored in the additional sheds erected to the west of the original sheds built by Wingfield.

Military activities at the crowded aerodrome at Shoreham were fraught with difficulties, not least because of the pace at which the trainee airmen had to be pushed through the school. On 23 June 1915, Lieutenant Ronald Morkill was killed when his aircraft fell to the ground.

Their Majesties King George and Queen Mary visited Shoreham on 3 November 1916. It was a purely military visit, but upon the arrival of the royal train, a considerable number of the inhabitants of the town and neighbourhood had gathered to give the king and queen a hearty welcome as they were driven along Buckingham Road. The whole distance from the station to the camp was lined on either side by Canadian soldiers, standing to attention. His Majesty the king visited Shoreham to inspect the camp again on 26 March 1918, but by this time, the outlook for the country had grown much darker.

The defences at the entrance to Shoreham harbour were added to in June 1918 with the construction of the 'mystery towers', so-called because of the secrecy surrounding the project at the time. They were to form part of a twelve-tower line of defence that was to have been erected in the Straits of Dover between Dungeness and Cap Gris Nez, each of the towers linked by steel boom nets designed to block the path for German U-boats.

The towers stood 180 feet from a base of around 190 feet, and 9,000 tons of concrete formed a honeycomb in a hexagonal shape rising in narrowing stages. This was topped by a 1,000 ton, 100-foot steel cylinder for around ninety men and supplies. The towers themselves housed submarine detection equipment, which was powered by its own special electricity generating facility. Gun emplacements were to be installed on top of each tower, and would be surrounded by minefields.

Two of the towers were almost completed and three more were at the half-way stage when, on the grey morning of 11 November, the bells rang out the glad tidings of Armistice. Two of the towers were completed after the war to allow for research, and on 12 September 1920, one of the towers was floated off to form what is now the Nab Tower on the Nab Sandbank off the Isle of Wight, replacing the former lightship, serving as a navigation station for the busy shipping lanes.

Amy Johnson with her Gipsy Moth *Jason* (G-AAZV), a month after her solo flight from England to Australia in May 1930. (Author's Collection)

CHAPTER 3

1919–1939
Between the Wars

Nos 1 and 2 Squadrons of the newly formed Canadian Air Force arrived at Shoreham from Upper Heyford, Oxfordshire, where they had been re-equipped with Sopwith Dolphins, SE5s, and DH-9s on 20 November 1918, nine days after the Armistice was signed. They spent several months testing and training on some of the sixty-five captured German aircraft that had been stored at the aerodrome. On 22 May 1919, Canadian ace pilot Major Albert Desbrisay Carter, DSO and Bar, MC, DFC, Croix de Guerre, of No. 2 Squadron, was test-flying a Fokker D.VII when one of the wings broke apart and the aircraft crashed in a field near Lancing College, killing him instantly. He was buried at Old Shoreham cemetery.

The Canadian government's decision not to retain an air force in peacetime led to both squadrons being disbanded in early 1920. The British government having lost interest in the post-war aerodrome, the freehold estate of around 147 acres was put up for auction on 6 December 1921, but having attracted no offers, was withdrawn from the market, and reverted back to grazing land for cattle. In the meantime, George Wingfield was in the process of trying to develop the Sussex County Aero Club from a barn and a building he used as a clubhouse on a piece of land called Easter's Field, on the south side of the railway line, but despite extensive advertising, he received little support.

Cecil Pashley, MBE, AFC, CFI, obtained his pilot's 'B' licence in 1920, when they were first instituted, and following a period of flying for the Central Aircraft Company of Northolt, he went into partnership with Frederick George Miles (who was in Reading at this time producing his own aircraft, a low wing cantilever monoplane called the Hawk). Miles had heard about Wingfield's failed attempt to revive the Sussex County Aero Club, and at the end of 1925, after being taught to fly by Pashley, he rented the barn in Easter's Field and, with his younger brother George, who had joined the team, used an Avro 504K to start a flying school and 'joyriding' business known as the Gnat Aero Company, where pupils were charged an hourly rate of £3 15s od for both dual and solo lessons of thirty-minute duration, with a minimum of forty hours being required within a six-month period. The student's and private pilot's licences at the time cost 1s 2½d.

However, the Air Ministry refused to license the field as a proper aerodrome, and so in 1926, Miles divided their operations and rented another field north of the railway, where a clubhouse and two new hangars were built. In May 1927, the new businesses were formally incorporated as limited companies: Southern Aircraft Ltd, which catered for aircraft repair and maintenance, and the Southern Aero Club, in which Pashley took an active role, and which concentrated on the leisurely pursuits of aviation as well as training new pilots. One of the aircraft Miles acquired was an Avro Baby, which he modified to turn it into an aerobatic sports aircraft he called the *Southern Martlet*, which was produced in 1929.

The first annual King's Cup Air Race, sponsored by King George V, started on 8 September 1922. The cross-country course of 810 miles was won the following day by Franklyn Leslie Barnard, chief pilot of Instone Air Line, in an Airco DH-4A (G-EAMU) named *City of York*, and the event led to a renewed interest in aviation, which steadily increased at Shoreham through the second half of the 1920s. Flying meetings and air shows returned to the aerodrome, and attracted famous flyers such as Sir Alan Cobham who, along with Air Vice-Marshal Sir Sefton Brancker, worked very hard to revive local municipal interest in Shoreham as an airport.

In mid-1928, Frederick Miles Senior, the owner of the Star Model laundry in nearby Portslade, and the source of much of his son's financing, was approached by the Mayor of Worthing to discuss acquiring the land for a municipal airport, and this led to a joint conference involving Brighton, Hove and Worthing.

By this time, the Miles brothers had started to produce their own aircraft designs and their single-seat biplane sports aircraft, the *Southern Martlet* (G-AAII) (one of six that would be built), took off from Shoreham on 10 July 1929. In October, pilot Edgar Percival made the first flight in the Hendy 281 Hobo (G-AAIG), a one-off single-seat light monoplane produced by the Hendy Aircraft Company.

The female aviator Amy Johnson landed her biplane for a brief stop at Shoreham on 30 August 1930, as part of her tour of the South Coast, where she received a civic reception and watched a small flying display.

Sir Alan Cobham, the famous pioneer of long-distance aviation, who, in 1932, started the National Aviation Day displays (which were often referred to as Cobham's Flying Circus), was engaged by the local authorities in 1930 to survey possible airfield sites in the area, and chose the original Shoreham field, which had been used until 1921, to be the municipal airport for the three towns. It already possessed key features for an aerodrome: a railway station on one side, a main road on the other, and the possibilities of operating seaplanes on the River Adur. However, the council took no action to develop a local airport, so Fred Miles persuaded his father to buy the disused site. Not long afterwards, Fred Miles went to South Africa, and his brother George took over the running of the company. When Fred returned, he set up a design office with his wife, Maxine 'Blossom', whom he had taught to fly. Their first aircraft, the single-seat Miles M.1 Satyr (G-ABVG), was produced in 1932, and led to the formation of the Miles Aircraft Company, based at Woodley aerodrome, near Reading.

Sir Alan Cobham returned to Shoreham on 6–7 August 1932, with his National Aviation Day Display, which consisted of a team of up to fourteen aircraft, ranging from single-seaters to modern airliners, and many skilled pilots.

In 1931, the go-ahead for the municipal airport was received, and George Wingfield commended the local authorities at a Southern Aero Club luncheon, at which he was an honoured guest on 9 May, for their shared vision of the future for Shoreham. The auspicious day was marked by a flying programme which included Fred Miles in his *Metal Martlet*, and a flypast of Martlets, Moths and Avians, a Bluebird, Cutty Sark, Desoutter, Widgeon, Redwing, Spartan and an autogiro (a forerunner of the helicopter).

Subsequently the authorities bought the airfield from Miles senior for £10,000, and, working to a budget of £31,000 for the terminal and hangars, architect Stavers Tiltman was brought in to design the terminal building and associated hangars, and James Bodel Ltd were engaged to carry out the construction work, which started in October 1934.

The Comper Swift (Gypsy III) made its widely anticipated first public appearance at Brooklands, having been entered by HRH the Prince of Wales for the tenth anniversary of Britain's premier cross-country air race – the King's Cup Race, which was run by the Royal Aero Club Records Racing and Rally Association. The two day event, which started on Friday 9 July 1932, saw new aircraft types such as the Arrow Active II (Gypsy III), a development of its predecessor; a Hermes 'B'; and the Percival 'Gull' (Hermes IV), a low-wing three-seater monoplane. The event was open to British pilots only, but that did include members of the Commonwealth.

On the first day of the cross-country air race, which was about 728 miles, the machines started at Brooklands and flew via Abingdon, Shoreham and Portsmouth to Whitchurch aerodrome at Bristol, where there was a compulsory stop of forty minutes. They then flew to Ratcliffe aerodrome, Leicester, via Birmingham (Castle Bromwich), Hooton and Manchester (Woodford), where there was another forty-minute compulsory stop at Leicester before the last stage of the first day's race – flying back to Brooklands via Ipswich municipal aerodrome and then Sywell aerodrome at Northampton. The control points were Bristol and Leicester; the other aerodromes were just turning points. The circuits flown over the two days totalled 1,223 miles.

The Prince of Wales (later Edward VIII/the Duke of Windsor) arrived at Shoreham on 4 July 1933 to open the new £100,000 lock and inaugurate the new lifeboat station at Shoreham-on-Sea. The aerodrome was a hive of activity for several months as building work was carried out, including the GV II VR2 hangar, which was erected by the firm of Boulton & Paul of London and Norfolk.

The new airport was ready for use by 1 September 1935, less than a year after work had been started on it. Railway Air Services had included Shoreham in its schedules, and the Southern Railway had reopened the old Bungalow Town Halt as Shoreham Airport. H. Milner Black, JP, the chairman's aid of the Airport Committee, invited the members and chief officials of the Brighton, Hove and Worthing town councils to pay an official visit. The occasion was more or less an official opening, and was marked by the arrival from Lympne of a large number of light aeroplanes in formation, while machines owned by Olley Air Services Ltd brought up the rear. The Croydon-based company had been appointed to manage the aerodrome, and was already running a Croydon–Shoreham–Deauville service, which started on 13 July. The old Southern Aero Club came under the control of Brooklands Aviation Group, and was renamed the South Coast Flying Club, retaining Cecil Pashley's services as its chief flying instructor, and membership of the clubhouse had passed the hundred mark.

Just a week later, on 7 September, Mr T. Rose won the King's Cup Air Race in a Miles Falcon with an average speed of 176.28 mph. For the first time the race consisted of two separate sections:

> Yesterday competitors flew in qualifying heats over a course of 947 miles, which took them over England, Scotland, Northern Ireland and Wales. The Duke of Kent's *Percival Mew Gull*, flown by Mr E. W. Percival, an Australian, which started from scratch, finished sixth, having attained a record average speed for the race of 208.51 mph.

In 1936, the Miles Company began producing training airplanes for the Air Ministry; the Miles Magister (a development of the Hawk) remained a standard trainer for the RAF throughout the Second World War, with more than 1,200 built. Fred Miles was also approached by Colonel Charles Lindbergh to build him a fast, long-range, light aeroplane for European business trips. This became the Mohawk, first flown in 1937.

The large crowds that had gathered on Empire Air Day, 23 May 1936, to view the flying were treated to an ad hoc display when an unlicensed pilot, Mr H. G. Aitchison, who had been a pupil at the Oxford University Air Squadron in 1931, but had been rejected due to an issue with his eyesight, took off in a De Havilland Moth (G-ABWL) without permission and proceeded to carry out some aerobatics which included several loops at around 1,500 feet, and then climbed to 3,000 feet and purposely put the aircraft into a spin. The aeroplane appeared to be spinning normally, but there was no change in its attitude or speed of rotation by the pilot. The machine impacted the ground. Aitchison was seriously injured, though very fortunate to survive at all. The Accident Investigation Bureau concluded, after examining the wreckage and finding no obvious faults, that, given his defective eyesight, the pilot had misjudged the height above ground.

On 13 June 1936, the exquisite art deco terminal building, which had been designed by architect Stavers Hessell Tiltman and built by James Bodel Ltd, was officially opened by the mayors Councillor Denne of Brighton, Councillor Loadsman of Hove, and Alderman Tree of Worthing. Alderman Tree was presented with a solid gold key to the doors by Tiltman. The final building construction costs amounted to £29,000, with £11,900 for ground works, and £8,300 for ancillary services, making a total cost to the local authorities of £49,200.

The building, which has a steel frame built on a concrete raft with brick walls rendered in 'Snowcrete', is situated on the south side of the airport and features a three-storey central pavilion with a porch and full-width canopy on two columns at ground-floor level and a recessed entrance. It is flanked by two two-storey wings southwards, projecting ends.

The internal decoration was in the 'moderne' style, and housed the administration offices, a customs hall, restaurant and bars, and the upper floors were reached by a double staircase.

A square air traffic control tower was erected on the roof, accessible by twin iron staircases. Only one hangar was built out of the four that the original plans provided for (and this is still in use today). A further two would be built in 1937.

In all, 100 aeroplanes from all parts of the country, and around thirty from the Continent, were parked on the airfield, and the two-day opening ceremony included an air display and, on the second day, hosted the first South Coast Air Trophy Race. Other buildings on site were a main hangar, workshops and six private lock-up hangars. With the completion of the terminal building, scheduled flying services were increased almost straightaway, with companies such as Railway Air Services, Southend-on-Sea-based Channel Air Ferries (previously Olley Air Services Ltd), Channel Island Airways, and Jersey Airways soon using the airport for destinations such as Bristol, Cardiff, Liverpool and Manchester, Jersey, Le Touquet and Deauville.

Shoreham was the staging point for the King's Cup Air Race in 1936, in which Amy Johnson was a competitor, but in 1937, the sense of another conflict was in the air when the Air Ministry opened the Martins School of Air Navigation to train RAF Volunteer Reserve personnel at the airport, and Bellman hangars were erected to house their De Havilland Tiger Moths, Hawker Harts and Hinds, and, later, Avro Ansons and Fairey Battles. Martins later officially became No. 16 Elementary and Reserve Flying Training School.

In May 1939 the last Empire Air Day was held at Shoreham, and the military aircraft present included the Vickers Vildebeest, Fairey Swordfish and Supermarine Walrus. In August 1939, Cecil Pashley, who, when war against Germany was declared, left for South Africa and trained many pilots under the Empire Air Training Scheme, was the honoured guest at a dinner to celebrate his thirty years of flying at Shoreham, where his remarkable record of 10,000 flying hours had been recorded; the majority of that was as an instructor.

Frederick Miles had said that Pashley had not followed ordinary success, but had gone quietly on with the work he liked best and had probably done much more for aviation in that way. In his reply, Pashley described his first solo flight with the Blériot for the benefit of those at the club who were about to go solo themselves; his impressions were mainly of considerable bewilderment, but after taxiing his aircraft for 'ages – several weeks', an early morning of complete calm was chosen for an initial flight. And very glad he was to get back on the ground. Among those who had sent congratulations were Messrs Grahame White, Gordon England and Handley Page. Other unofficial speakers were Mrs Pashley, Flight Lieutenant Rose, and Councillor Andrews, the chairman of the airport committee, who said, 'Shoreham Municipal aerodrome was shortly to be considerably extended and provided with a blind approach system.'

Passenger air services to Jersey, Birmingham and Liverpool had been in operation since 1938, but with the outbreak of the Second World War on 3 September 1939, international airline operators were moved from London (Croydon) Airport to Shoreham. Sabena, DDL, KLM and the predecessor of British Airways, Imperial Airways, were among the companies which flew to destinations including Copenhagen, Amsterdam, Malmö and Brussels.

The aircraft had high-visibility orange neutrality paint but had to be covered with camouflage netting overnight. Croydon's airport traffic was also rerouted to Shoreham, which became the terminal for flights from the neutral countries of Belgium, France, Denmark and the Netherlands. Grumman Albatrosses,

Armstrong-Whitworth Ensigns and old Handley-Page HP-42s flew to destinations such as North Africa, Egypt, India and Europe.

The last Empire Air Day had been held at Shoreham on 20 May 1939, and all club and private flying soon ceased. The new airport terminal building and hangars were given a coat of heavy green paint as camouflage – the distinctive features of all wartime RAF stations – to deceive or confuse the enemy.

CHAPTER 4

1940–1945
The Second World War

With the German invasion of France and the Low Countries in 1940, the passenger traffic to and from Shoreham ceased, and the airport was requisitioned by the Air Ministry in June 1940 in the Tangmere sector. There were already a number of RAF airfields across East and West Sussex, and so, despite the tendency to flooding in wet weather, which had always been a problem, Shoreham's main use was to provide the earliest possible landing place for badly damaged aircraft of all types which had managed to limp back to the English coast from sorties across the Channel. The RAF station at Shoreham was an administrative base only, and comprised station headquarters, motor transport section, sick quarters and a few wooden billets; the area is now occupied by Parklands, and part of Wilmot Road.

The railway station was closed, and, as with all other airfields across the country, the buildings were disguised by camouflage netting, and the airport terminal building and hangars were given a coat of 'heavy green' paint. Members of the Lancing College OTC assisted in the digging of trenches on and around the airfield. The airfield was also defended by as many as eleven pillboxes, of which three remain: one overlooking the access road to the old ferry bridge, one facing south giving wide cover from the embankment, and another further down the path. There was also a field gun and light anti-aircraft emplacements around its perimeter, and at least one Pickett-Hamilton Fort; this was more commonly known as a 'Pop-up Pillbox', a 9–10-inch-thick concrete cylinder, 9 feet in diameter, buried in the ground, with a concrete inner sleeve that could be raised or lowered via either a hydraulic jack or a hand pump, which formed the 'pop-up' element, and could accommodate two or three men armed with rifles.

An early air gunnery simulator was built inside a dome that was erected on the north-west side of the airfield, and was used to train many hundreds of RAF Regiment gunners. Inside the dome, which was around 20 feet in diameter, there were two rooms. In one was a large screen painted to resemble the local skyline with the downs and Adur Valley, and in the other (behind the screen) a projector displayed a silhouette of German aircraft against the sky. The trainee gunners were given imitation guns that shone a small spotlight at the exact point where they were firing. Accompanied by the soundtrack of a firing shot, which was played whenever the trigger was pulled, the instructor was able to assess their accuracy. After the war the dome became a drill hall for 1440 Squadron ATC, and is one of only six left in the UK.

In Shoreham town, like the rest of the UK, the street lighting was turned off. White lines were painted on roadways, and black-and-white kerb stones fitted onto the pavements to assist traffic and pedestrians when the blackout was introduced. Road signs were taken down or turned around to confuse any invading armies. Trenches were dug in the playing fields of the Shoreham grammar school in Pond Lane (now Greenacres), and a large searchlight, an anti-aircraft gun, and heavy machine gun emplacements were installed, as well as a barrage balloon which was floated from time to time. The school's gymnasium was used as the headquarters of No. 9 (Shoreham) Platoon of the Sussex Home Guard.

The ARP would carry out regular nightly street patrols, enforcing the blackout rules, and would cordon off any area where an unexploded bomb was found or gas from a ruptured mains or gas attack could be smelt.

De Havilland Leopard LN-TVT, 1952. (Author's Collection)

The Territorial Army gunners of the 113th Regiment of Field Artillery, which was based in Worthing, set up a field headquarters in Buckingham Park, and their 25-pound guns were dug in, and ranged on to the airport and Shoreham beach, where it was thought the enemy landings might occur. Shoreham beach consisted mainly of wooden buildings and old railway carriages (some occupied by some famous actors and actresses), which were blown up by the military to make it clear to fight the Germans and to shell them from the Downs. The beach was then mined, barbed-wire entanglements set up, and a line of concrete blocks placed all along the open stretches of coastline.

The 344th Battery, 15th Coastal Artillery Group, which was part of Eastern Command's coastal defences, set up at Shoreham in June, and the Shoreham Redoubt was taken over, a brick searchlight tower was built, and two 6-inch naval guns were installed on the beach nearby. The South Down golf course, which had also been taken over for the war effort, was obliterated by tank exercises, and the clubhouse was used for target practice (the club never reopened after the war).

The Observer Corps played a vital role in identifying and range finding incoming aircraft, and were an important part of Britain's defence network. Their skills were used by the anti-aircraft gunners, who needed to know the height, distance, speed and heading for proximity of the fuses on shells. They were also able to inform Fighter Command about enemy aircraft returning from attacks on the city, enabling them to engage them as they fled across the Channel.

Trenches and defence ditches were dug out around the airfield, mainly by members of Lancing College who were sent down to assist the air force ground crews. Lancing College had been taken over for a while by General Montgomery as his headquarters before the Royal Navy took control and established it as HMS *King Arthur*, a RNVR (Royal Naval Volunteer Reserve) training depot, for the rest of the war. The Sussex Pad was taken over and used as the officers' mess, and Ricardo's (the Dolphin engine production factory) for the sergeants' mess, which did provide some sleeping accommodation, but all the other servicemen were billeted around town.

The aircraft designs of F. G. Miles were often technologically and aerodynamically advanced for their time, and the M.20 emergency production fighter was a 'quick-to-build' alternative to the contemporary Hawker Hurricanes and Supermarine Spitfires. However, when it was realised that, due to dispersal of manufacturing, the Luftwaffe's bombing of the factories didn't adversely affect their production, production of the M.20 didn't go ahead.

One of the first incidents in the war was when three Polish airmen, who had escaped from their homeland, flew across Europe and landed at Shoreham airport.

On 10 February 1940, a lone Dornier Do17 droned over Shoreham, crossing the airfield at low height. It was engaged by the ground defences, and no bombs were dropped, but it tested the efficiency of the battery and airfield armaments. In May 1940, 225 Squadron (which had been re-formed from 614A Squadron in October 1939) moved in to the aerodrome, and patrolled along the coast of Hampshire and the Isle of Wight with their Lysander aircraft, watching for the expected German invasion fleet. The squadron also provided air-sea rescue cover from 6 May 1941.

Following the evacuation of Allied forces from Dunkirk, many intense air battles were fought in the skies above West Sussex during August and September 1940. During the morning of *Adler Tag* (Eagle Day) – 13 August – Oberleutnant Paul Temme of Jagdgeschwader 2, 'Richthofen', crash-landed his Messerschmitt Bf 109E (5068) in a stubble field at New Salts Farm after being shot down by Sergeant J. P. Mills in a Hawker Hurricane of 43 Squadron, which had been scrambled from Tangmere to intercept a large formation of Ju 88s, Bf 109s, and Bf 110s that was approaching from the south near Littlehampton. Temme was handed into the custody of the RAF regiment, and as a prisoner of war, was subsequently interned in Canada.

The Fighter Interception Unit (FIU) of the RAF arrived at Shoreham with their Hurricanes on 18 September 1940, after their base at Tangmere was bombed. The

Miles Gemini G-ALZG at Shoreham. (Author's Collection)

unit had been initially set up to evaluate technological advances such as airborne interception (AI) equipment (an onboard interception radar) and other operational innovations, to counter the increasing number of night raids by the Luftwaffe, but had also achieved the first airborne radar intercepted kill in history on the night of 22/23 July when a Blenheim Mk 1F from Tangmere, while on a patrol over the Sussex coast, was directed to a possible intercept by the controller at Poling Chain Home radar station, who reported an incoming raid. The onboard AI responded, and the operator was able to guide the pilot until he made a visual sighting of an enemy aircraft, a Dornier Do 17, which they fired upon, striking the fuselage and one of the engines. The bomber crashed into the sea, and its crew were later rescued.

The airmen were found billets at Lancing, and the officers at the Sussex Pad, and they began defence patrols the next day. Four days later, the pilots took the Hurricanes back to Tangmere, and five Bristol Blenheim Mk Is and two Mk IVs were allotted to the unit for night patrols testing out the newly fitted AI radar. On the following day, a Miles Magister was delivered for communications work.

At dusk on 8 October, the airport was attacked by three enemy bombers. They approached from inland, dropped bombs on the north environs of Shoreham, Worthing and Lancing, and then machine-gunned the airport buildings. No one was hurt, although many got a soaking from jumping to the safety of dykes and ditches.

The FIU carried out night patrols, calibration flights for ground-controlled interception (GCI), gunnery tests at sea, flare shooting and ZZ landings (a series of radio bearings that assisted a pilot to land in bad visibility). The unit was moved in small parties from 26 to 31 January 1941 to RAF Ford for permanent service, but on 27 January, the *Daily Express* published a strip describing the infrared telescope, which at the time was a new and secret piece of equipment that was being researched and tested by the FIU. The unit was joined at the airfield by No. 422 Flight, a special Hawker Hurricane night-fighter unit formed at Shoreham on October, but was shortly afterwards moved to Cranage, near Crewe, where it was renumbered 96 Squadron on 18 December 1940.

On 1941, the grass landing strip was extended, the 800-yard north-to-south runway being too short for the numbers and types of aircraft that were arriving, damaged US 8th Air Force Liberators, as well as Spitfires, Whitleys and Thunderbolts. To facilitate the extension, the New Salts Farm Road embankment, which formed the western boundary, was levelled, and the old airfield was incorporated along with a strip of land in the south-west corner, providing a 1,200-yard run on 04/22 (north-east to south-west).

Miles Gemini G-AKFY at Shoreham, 6 May 1955. (Author's Collection)

The FIU left Shoreham for RAF Ford on 1 February, but it wasn't long before the Luftwaffe started to make more frequent visits to the airfield, and carried out sporadic bombing and strafing attacks. On 13 March, seven Me 109s dropped HE (high-explosive) bombs but with little effect, and not long after, two Me 109s strafed the hangars and buildings, but with no casualties reported. Further bombing attacks by lone enemy fighters occurred in the following weeks, but the worst was to come when five air raids were carried out on the night of 8 September, and it was the fourth, heaviest attack that caused the most damage to the airfield, temporarily putting it out of action. The terminal building was not damaged, but the main hangars were destroyed, and the GV II VR2 hangar was badly damaged; all the cladding was blown off but the framework was left intact. To protect the ground crews from the inclement weather, two blister hangars were erected under the frame, enabling the hangar to continue in service. The Nissen hut in front of the hangar, where maintenance crews waited for returning aircraft, was not damaged. The last air raid of Shoreham in 1941 took place on 19 December, during which ACW Phyllis Hicks (aged twenty) of the WAAF and Corporal Harcourt Dowdeswell (aged twenty-eight) of the RAFVR were killed.

In December, Shoreham also became a base for part of the newly formed 277 Air Sea Rescue 'Kiwi' Squadron, which was allocated to 11 Group, Fighter Command. A detachment comprising Westland Lysanders and Supermarine Walrus flying boats arrived (other detachments being sent to Hawkinge and Martlesham Heath), and operated from GV II VR2 hangar, to cover the area between the south-east of England and the French coast, one of the busiest areas around the British coast during the Second World War. The squadron would be involved in the rescue of nearly 600 airmen from the Channel. Being called out in any weather, day or night, the Walrus aircraft (which was also referred to as Shagbat or sometimes steam-pigeon – the latter name coming from the steam produced by water striking the hot Pegasus engine) frequently alighted in enemy coastal waters to pick up ditched Allied airmen from their dinghies, sometimes putting down in minefields where rescue launches could not venture. Once back at home, the casualties would be transferred into waiting ambulances for ferrying to hospital.

The Lysanders were used primarily to spot downed airmen and drop dinghies, and, being such extremely manoeuvrable aircraft, capable of taking off and landing on short stretches of ground, were also used for the setting down and picking up secret agents of the Special Operations Executive, the exploits of whom were subsequently featured in a drama series on BBC television, deep in enemy territory.

277 Squadron lost one of their Walrus aircraft on 21 July 1942 when it crashed into the sea 2 miles off Worthing Pier, but Flight Lieutenant Tom Fletcher, DFM, and his crew escaped unhurt. On another occasion, Fletcher found a number of aircrew in the sea while spotting from a Lysander, and directed RAF high-speed launches to rescue them. Up to this time he had saved nine men.

On 14 December 1942, six men were spotted adrift on a raft 10 miles east of Dover, and Fletcher landed a Walrus (W3097) in the rough seas even though he knew that it would be impossible to take off again. In failing light, he made three passes, picking up the men one by one, although several of them were swept from the raft. His aircraft was shipping water, and by the time it was completely dark, Fletcher reluctantly abandoned the search and taxied back towards Dover, a journey that took him almost two hours, only to be met by the harbour master, who reprimanded him for not getting permission to bring the sinking aircraft into port. He also received a bar to his DFM. The rescued crew he had gone to such lengths to rescue were German sailors.

277 Squadron regrouped at Shoreham from April 1944 until October, when it left for Hawkinge, and by then it also operated Supermarine Spitfires and Sea Otters, Boulton-Paul Defiants, and a Barnes Wallis-designed Vickers-Armstrong Warwick.

The 4th and 5th Landing Flotillas of the Royal Navy were to have arrived in secrecy at Shoreham in early August to prepare for the Allied raid on Dieppe

Percival Prince IIIB G-AMLZ at Shoreham, 15 May 1955. (Author's Collection)

in 1942, but due to a miscalculation of the tides, most of the small vessels ran aground, and were visible to everyone. The raid, code-named Operation Jubilee, was planned in the terminal building at Shoreham, and in the late summer, a Combined Operations landing craft base was established at Butt's Baltic Wharf on Aldrington Basin (also referred to as Portslade Basin) at Shoreham. Commissioned as an independent command with the ship's name HMS *Lizard* on 7 October 1942, the base provided training in seamanship and survival skills for men of the Royal Marines and Royal Navy to prepare them for their hazardous duties as landing craft crews, and used the facilities for the landing craft tank (LCT) available in Shoreham harbour. The final planning for the launch of the operation was carried out at HMS *King Alfred* (Lancing College).

The ground crews at the airfield were stretched to the limit on the day of the operation when several Hurricanes from Nos 3 and 245 squadrons, which had been badly shot up by the ground defences at Dieppe, landed for immediate repairs and refuelling. The aircraft were in and out all day long, some making four or five sorties each.

The command of Shoreham passed to the RNAS station at RAF Ford on 25 November, and in December, 2762 Squadron, RAF Regiment, took over the vital role of airfield defence. Throughout the war, more than eight RAF Regiment squadrons came and went, each on short stay postings.

The airport's biggest raid of the war occurred on 13 February 1943, when the control tower was hit and the other building set on fire, but otherwise no significant damage was incurred. On the night of 10/11 April 1943, thanks to the wonders of wireless radio, preparations had been made to rescue the crew of a Stirling Mk III bomber (BF455) of 75 Squadron, which had been damaged by anti-aircraft fire over its target, and was being escorted by Spitfires as she limped back across the English Channel. She ran out of fuel, eventually crashing into the sea 3 miles off Shoreham, where a Walrus was already waiting for her. The crew, led by Flight Sergeant Rothschild, were rescued by dinghy, but the Walrus collided with it, and the crew dropped back in the sea. No one suffered ill effects except for Sergeant Grainger, the flight engineer, who was in shock.

On another occasion in 1943, one of the Walrus floatplanes was intercepted by fifteen Me 109s; the top mainplane was hit and caught fire, and the aircraft landed heavily and sank, but the crew were picked up by another Walrus and flown back to Shoreham.

After the danger of daylight air raids had passed, a Walrus would take off from Shoreham airport and fly eastwards along the coast, and as it passed each town the 'All Clear' sirens would go off. It was affectionately known as the 'Singer', because its sound reminded people of a sewing machine.

A Martin B-26C Marauder (41-34703 – RJ-C) of the USAAF crash-landed on the South Downs while attempting emergency landing at Shoreham on 2 August 1943. There were no crew casualties but the aircraft was damaged beyond repair.

The first operational Supermarine Sea Otters were delivered to 277 Squadron on November 1943. With their longer range and greater load-carrying capability, they were intended to replace the Walruses, but with demand being so high for the production of Spitfires, the Supermarine company was working flat out, and deliveries of Sea Otters were staggered. Nonetheless, by May 1944, the squadron had carried out 498 rescue missions.

For the damaged aircraft that used the airfield for emergency landings, it was not without drama; there would often be holes and bits missing from the struggling aircraft, and fabric flapping in the slipstream, and landing into the prevailing wind meant that the bridge was their marker for their final approach. For some, the urgency was so great that they dispensed with any such preliminaries, and touched down at the first possible moment. On one occasion a Hurricane failed to stop and ended up in the river, and a Blenheim bomber also attempting to land did not make the airfield and crashed near Lancing College.

Following America's entry into the war, massed formations of Boeing B-17 Flying Fortresses and Consolidated B-24 Liberators would rendezvous for their missions,

Miles Whitney Straight F-APPZ. (Author's Collection)

and circle high over Shoreham before flying on to their targets, the sheer numbers of aircraft producing condensation trails so dense that they made the sky appear overcast. Shoreham was an emergency landing point for these large aircraft, too, and after repairs were made, the difficulty was in flying them out again.

On 11 February 1944, three B-17s from 359th Squadron of the 303rd Bomber Group, based at Molesworth, Cambridgeshire, were forced to make emergency landings at Shoreham after a raid on Germany. Two which were low on fuel landed successfully, but the third, *Scorchy* (42-31314 BS-M), which had been damaged, suffered brake failure upon landing. Its port wing tip tore into the guardhouse on the north side of the airfield, and the other wing tip hit No. 4 gun post, severely injuring an armourer. The aircraft came to rest with a broken fuselage, two crumpled wings, and the tailplane torn off, but the crew escaped with relatively minor injuries.

HMS *Lizard* provided the support base for the large number of vessels that crowded into Shoreham harbour in the run-up to Operation Neptune on D-Day, 6 June 1944. The invasion barges were moored by the Old Shoreham toll bridge, and were kept under camouflaged netting. Soldiers were billeted around town and in parts of Southlands hospital for a short time, and their tanks, guns, lorries and equipment were parked in the roads and lanes above the town. This was all part of Assault Force 'S', which had assembled at the ports of Newhaven, Shoreham, and Portsmouth. Once loaded, the flotillas sailed to rendezvous at Spithead,

Avro Anson G-ALIH, the test bed for EKCO Electronics of Southend-on-Sea, at Shoreham in 1959. (Author's Collection)

Portsmouth, on the morning of 5 June, where they prepared for the Channel crossing to Sword Beach, Normandy. The airport was also in a constant flurry of activity, and on 26 April, in preparation for the Normandy landings, became host to the newly formed 345 (Free French) fighter squadron of Spitfire Mk Vbs and Mk IXs, which operated out of two blister hangars at the northern end of the airfield, and carried out operational sorties from until August 1944, including three missions on D-Day.

It was during 1943 and 1944 that Sussex towns and villages suffered most heavily from enemy bombing raids, and despite some thirty-seven raids on Shoreham and Southwick, involving high-explosive bombs, oil bombs and incendiaries, causing seventeen deaths and 108 injuries, this number was marginal compared with nearby towns such as Brighton. However, several incidents were recorded involving the German doodlebugs – the V-1 flying bombs.

On 4 July 1944, a Spitfire from 277 Squadron shot down a doodlebug over Beachy Head, the pilot having to use the emergency boost in order to catch it up in the attack; the squadron had previously claimed two destroyed on 30 June (and five in all throughout the summer). Witness accounts state that on another occasion, a doodlebug was chased down and then 'nudged' by the wing tip of a British fighter, and observed it veering back out to sea. The practice of 'nudging' or 'tipping' involved physical contact, but caused damage to the pursuing aircraft. As it took a very steep and fast dive for a Spitfire to catch up with the rocket, it was

De Havilland DH 89A Rapide G-AKRN of East Anglian Flying Services Ltd of Southend-on-Sea. (Author's Collection)

Shoreham-by-Sea station with an M7 push-pull (30049) in 1952. (John Ford)

found that by moving in slightly above it, and placing the wing just above that of the rocket, the airflow over the rocket's wing was spoilt enough for it to bank out of control, particularly as it had no ailerons to counteract the movement.

345 Squadron left Shoreham for Deanland, near Lewes, on 16 August; things were beginning to wind down. A freak accident occurred on 16 August when a Spitfire from 277 Squadron collided with a truck on the perimeter road while coming in to land; the aircraft lost its undercarriage, but belly-landed safely on the airfield, and the pilot, Flight Lieutenant Adams, was unhurt. Another accident involving a Spitfire from 277 Squadron as it approached the airfield to land occurred on 18 September, when it hit the roof of a train and lost its undercarriage. Like the previous accident, the aircraft skidded to a halt on the grass and the pilot, Warrant Officer Bill Gadd, emerged unhurt.

The Air Ministry Film Unit arrived at Shoreham on 26 September to make a documentary about dinghy-dropping, among other ASR activities, and used 277 Squadron for the feature. Not long after, the squadron transferred to Warmwell and Hawkinge, and Shoreham airfield became much quieter. The last big incident at Shoreham occurred on 5 November, when a doodlebug was shot down by a Spitfire and fell on to the allotments opposite the park in Eastern Avenue. The resulting explosion blew out many windows, and damage was caused to some properties, but casualties with only minor injuries were reported.

Shoreham played out the remainder of the war as a satellite airfield for RAF Nether Wallop from March 1945, but was seldom used.

CHAPTER 5

1946–1959
Post-War and Recovery

In 1946, the airfield was handed back to civil flying, being made available from 1 January, but as with the end of the First World War, its recovery was slow. Cecil Pashley, who had been commissioned in the RAFVR for the duration of the war, returned to Shoreham in May. Within weeks he had revived the South Coast Flying Club, although it wasn't until April 1949 that it obtained a licence to serve light lunches, snacks and hot beverages on the premises.

On 29 June 1946, the airport was officially reopened for civil flying, and the occasion was marked by an air display, but over the next few years, the few attempts to operate scheduled services and air shows at Shoreham all failed, mainly due to the lack of a tarmac runway, the airfield being prone to flooding, and the condition of the buildings and hangars, which still bore the scars of the bombings during the war.

The Brookside Flying Group was formed during the latter months of 1947, operating a single Miles Hawk (G-AKRJ), which had been purchased for £350 in April 1948, plus annual insurance of £70. The club had a membership of around thirty people, mainly ex-servicemen, but, with flying charges of £4 per hour, not many could afford it, so they formed their own group, with profits from any of their activities going into the group funds.

An RAF Meteor, on a training flight from its base at Thorney Island, crashed into the sea west of Shoreham on 27 August 1948. The Shoreham lifeboat and RAF tenders from Newhaven put out, and two other Meteors circled the position where the missing plane was last seen. The lifeboat was directed by radio to search an area 1 mile south of Shoreham harbour, where the wreckage was found. The pilot was presumed killed.

On the morning of 29 January 1949, two members of the club, Herbert C. Pitcher and Frank Denton, arrived at Shoreham with the intention of flying 'RJ', but a heavy mist covered the airfield. Preflight checks were carried out, and at 1230 hours the mist had cleared, and they taxied the aircraft to the pumps for

A night departure from Shoreham airport (B.206S) on 31 March 1967. (Author's Collection)

Avro Anson G-AHKX of Meridian Air Maps Ltd around 1963. (Nick Denbow)

refuelling. They took off at 1256 hours and headed in a south-westerly direction. Observers on the ground watched the aircraft enter a turn to the starboard which continued through three or four complete circles, losing height all the while. The Hawk straightened out at low altitude, but after a few hundred yards, crashed into the water. The Shoreham lifeboat was launched straightaway, but upon reaching the downed aircraft, found that both occupants had already drowned and were still strapped in by their safety belts. After the crash, another Miles Hawk (G-AKRM) was purchased, which they operated until the group folded in early 1951. 'RM' passed into other hands, but crashed near Chester in 1953.

It wasn't until 1949 that the fortunes of the airport would see a change for the better, when East Anglian Flying Services, based in Southend-on-Sea, used Shoreham as an additional stop on some of their services to Jersey. On Sunday 29 May 1949, Air Marshal Sir Alan Lees, AOC-in-C (Air Officer Commanding in Chief), Reserve Command, arrived in his Avro Anson C-19, and there then followed some formation flying by four Spitfires of 615 Squadron, RAuxAF (Royal Auxiliary Air Force) – bumps notwithstanding – rounded off by a dashing beat-up of the airfield, and individual aerobatics. Squadron Leader Marsh also demonstrated the amazing little dual-control Saunders-Roe (Saro) 'Skeeter' helicopter. In buffeting wind, he repeated the performance he had given at Sywell on the previous weekend by unhooking a

Beagle B.206S at Shoreham, around 1965, just out of production. (Nick Denbow)

ring from a post and, to everyone's delight, replacing it, and by way of an encore, he followed with another party trick – that of landing on a lorry. The afternoon ended on the high note on which it had opened – with some excellent formation flying and a strafe by four Gloster Meteor Mk IIIs of 500 Squadron, RAuxAF.

The municipal hangar alongside the terminal building, which was damaged during the war, was repaired in 1950, and on 28 May, an air display of Supermarine Spitfires and Seafires, Gloster Meteors and an American Grumman Mallard was followed by other aircraft types, including Tiger Moths and Chipmunks, Ansons, Auster J/I Autocrats, Percival Procters and a Bristol Type 170 Mk 21 Freighter (G-AIME), to herald in a new era for Shoreham airport.

By the early 1950s, Shoreham had started to become well known again as an air racing and air display venue, and on 28 May, the Sussex Wing of the Air Training Corps held an RAF open day at Shoreham. The crowd of over 25,000 people were treated to a comprehensive programme of ambitious air displays, which included members of the 14th Parachute Regiment (TA) jumping from a captive balloon, formation flying by De Havilland Tiger Moths and Chipmunks, Avro Ansons from three reserve schools, Spitfires of 615 Squadron (RAuxAF), Seafires of 1832 Squadron (RNVR), and Meteors of 500 Squadron (RAuxAF). This was the first British jet fighter and the Allies' first operational jet aircraft.

The formation events were interspersed with items such as glider aerobatics, a variety of 'Chip-munkey' tricks performed by Flying Officer H. G. Hubbard, RAFVR, and the bombing of a moving target by a Tiger Moth. Mock bombing and strafing sequences were to become a hallmark for Shoreham air shows. Floor shows included marching by the bands of the 6th Cadet Regiment (RA), and the Sussex Wing of the Air Training Corps giving various displays.

Fifty-one entrants took part in the *Daily Express* Challenge Trophy, which took place on 22 September 1951 (after being postponed from 6 August because of adverse weather). The international handicap contest was run over a 186-mile course from Shoreham along the coast to Newhaven Lighthouse, then across country to Whitstable in Kent and back to the finishing line at Brighton West Pier.

The race attracted many well-known racing pilots, including five of the six members of the 'Throttle-Benders Union' – the unofficial brotherhood of regular participants in British air races: Tony Cole in a Comper Swift (G-ABUS), Fred Dunkerley in a Miles Gemini (G-AKDC), Ron Paine in a Miles Hawk Speed Six (G-ADGP), Squadron Leader James Rush in a Miles Falcon-Six (G-AECC), and Nat Somers in a Gemini III (G-AKDC). Three women pilots also entered: Mrs 'Peggy' Grace in a Taylorcraft Plus D, Miss Lettice Curtis in her own Wicko G.M.i, and Mrs Zita Irwin in the Windmill Theatre's Percival Proctor.

A Jodel D.117, G-ATIZ, on 25 June 1966, with a Gemini in the background. (Nick Denbow)

Hiller 360 UH 12E helicopter G-ATVN at Shoreham in October 1967. (Nick Denbow)

Beagle B.206 G-ATHO at Shoreham in 1966. (Nick Denbow)

Foreign competitors who took part were SAS pilot Captain Jan Christie of Norway; Ladislav Marmol, the well-known Czech sailplane pilot; Jean Lignel, the French designer (in one of his own machines, the Lignel 46); Jacques Garnier, of France, in a Norecrin; P. Genin, of Switzerland, flying a Bonanza; and G. A. Ferrari and Count Leonardo Bonzi, both of Italy, each in one of the new Italian Ambrosini S7s. The gruelling race was won by Hugh Kendall in a Chilton DWI monoplane (G-AFGI).

In 1952, Fred Miles moved back to Shoreham from Redhill airport with his wife to set up their aviation component fabrication business, operating from the workshops inside the municipal hangar, and also established the Southern Aero Club. They were later joined by his brother George, who had been working for Airspeed, and Grahame Gates as their chief project designer. In the following year, the company gained two new directors: Jack Angell from Bristol Engine Division, and Mrs O. M. Wadlow, who had been associated with the company since its Reading days and had been its secretary since it began operations at Redhill. Plans to move their plastics division from Redhill were also in hand, and the consolidated company, F. G. Miles Ltd, was set to become a major player in the aircraft industry.

A major refurbishment of the main hangars was carried out in the spring; the over blister was removed to form part of an extension to the hangar in the

Beagle A-61 Terrier G-ASAX at Shoreham on 25 June 1966. (Nick Denbow)

Rollason Druine D-62B Condor G-ATOH at Shoreham on 25 June 1966. In the background is the Air Gunnery Training Dome. (Nick Denbow)

south-east corner of the airfield. One of the over blister hangars on the northern boundary was dismantled and incorporated into the extension to create one large hangar (which would be used by Miles). Most of the refurbishment of the hangars was completed by mid-1952.

Shoreham was the starting point again for the 183-mile *Daily Express* South Coast Air Race on 2 August 1952. The majority of the aircraft were quite well known, having raced on many occasions before. There were eleven Proctors and Jean Batten's historic Gull (G-ADPR), flown by Group Captain Douglas Bader; six Taylorcraft Plus Ds, including the King's Cup winner; and one each of Austers, Autocrat, Autocar and Aiglet Trainer. As usual, bad weather delayed the start, but the winner out of the forty-six entrants was Wing Commander Robert Henry McIntosh (All-Weather Mac), chief pilot for Airwork Ltd, in a Proctor I (G-AHGA).

East Anglian Flying Services Ltd reintroduced daily scheduled flights from Shoreham in 1952, using four De Havilland DH-89 Dragon Rapides (which were later replaced with DH-104 Doves), two Proctors, two Tiger Moths, and one Auster, for their Ipswich–Southend–Rochester–Shoreham–Paris service, their Ipswich–Southend–Rochester–Shoreham–Channel Islands service, and (as from

Aero 145 G-ASWK refuelling at Shoreham on 25 June 1966. (Nick Denbow)

Taylorcraft Auster V G-AGLK at Shoreham on 25 June 1966. (Nick Denbow)

1 June) their Ipswich–Southend–Ostend and Ipswich–Southend–Calais services. It is noteworthy that Jackie Moggridge, the famous ATA pilot, flew for EAFS in 1956 (she would later become the first female airline captain in the country, flying the Channel Airways Doves, also into Shoreham, and was the first woman in the country to break the sound barrier). The company ceased operations at Shoreham in 1961, a year before officially changing its name to Channel Airways, but was considered to be one of the most successful and long-running airlines and most entitled to be considered as Shoreham's own airline.

The first flight of the Miles M.77 Sparrowjet – a twin-engined jet-powered racing aircraft capable of well over 200 mph, and the first British light aircraft to use jet power – took place at Shoreham on 14 December 1953. The aircraft was a conversion of the Miles M.5 Sparrowhawk (G-ADNL), which was carried out by Fred Dunkerley's Oldham Tyre Cord Company in January 1951, and was flown by Dunkerley in air races during the Goodyear Air Challenge Trophy at Shoreham on 28 August 1954.

The Chelsea College of Aeronautical Engineering set up their premises on the southern edge of the field (now known as Northbrook College), a second campus being at Worthing.

Cecil Pashley celebrated more than forty years as a flying instructor. He had logged over 17,000 flying hours, was one of the best known of the country's

Wassmer WA-41 Super Baladou G-AVEU at Shoreham in October 1967. (Nick Denbow)

Piper PA-18-140 Cherokee G-ATOK at Shoreham in October 1967. (Nick Denbow)

Percival Proctor P.28 G-AIED looking abandoned at Shoreham on 25 June 1966. (Nick Denbow)

surviving aviation pioneers, and still played an active role with the South Coast Flying Club after it was transformed into the (earlier) Southern Aero Club in 1957.

One of the most important projects for F. G. Miles Ltd was a contract from Rolls-Royce in July 1955 to provide a test bed for their compact RB108 engine, which was intended primarily for use as a VTOL (vertical take-off and landing) engine, providing upwards thrust rather than horizontal propulsion. A Gloster Meteor FR9 (VZ608) was modified by Miles for ground effect trials to see where dust and debris 'went' as a result of the downward thrust of the engine in the vertical position. The data was provided for the design of the Short SC-I vertical take-off research aircraft.

On 2 April 1955, the first prototype Hurel-Dubois HD-32 (F-WGVG) was demonstrated at Shoreham. Airlines represented included BEA (whose chief executive, Peter Masefield, flew the aircraft), BOAC, ANA, Hunting-Clan and Skyways. BOAC's observer was Mr Whitney Straight, deputy chairman. Following the Shoreham demonstration, the aircraft left for Blackpool airport the following day, where it was flown by Skyways' chief pilot, continuing – at the request of Aer Lingus – to Dublin.

The Southern Aero Club suffered its first fatality on 16 August 1955, when an ATC cadet crashed a Miles M.14A Hawk Trainer III (G-AITS) while beating up his girlfriend's house near Hurstpierpoint. The aircraft was written off.

Piper PA-24-250 Comanche G-ARIN at Shoreham on 25 June 1966. (Nick Denbow)

British Aircraft Corporation Beagle B.206 G-AVHO at Shoreham in 1966. (Nick Denbow)

Irish Aviation Services Beagle B.206 EI-APO at Shoreham in 1966. (Nick Denbow)

Fred Miles at the controls of the S.E.5a, which was built for the 1966 film *The Blue Max*. (Donald Gray)

In August 1956, Miles were constructing the experimental prototype of the HDM 106. The venture, in partnership with Hurel-Dubois, was to modify the Miles Aerovan HDM 105 by conjoining the aerodynamic advantages of the high aspect ratio wing (which was what Hurel-Dubois excelled in) with a small but capacious fuselage (fifteen passengers or a 1½ tons of freight), with big rearward-opening doors, thus combining in a small vehicle the commercial advantages of freighting as well as passenger carrying.

Fred Dunkerley piloted the Miles Sparrowjet to victory in the King's Cup Race in 1957, achieving a top speed of 228 mph; the 2nd, 3rd, and 5th places were all won by Miles aircraft.

Other projects that saw the decade out for Miles included modifications to the Miles Gemini, which was flown for Shell Aviation by Group Captain Bader, and initial designs for the replacements for the Miles Messenger and Gemini aircraft, but financial difficulties cast a shadow over the future of the company.

Meridian Air Maps (another company with Miles' involvement) began operating their aerial survey work from Shoreham with a Miles M.57 Aerovan Mk IV, but two tragic accidents occurred in 1957: an Aerovan (G-AISF) crashed on take-off from

Beagle D5/180 Husky G-ASBV in 1962, the first to be powered by a 180-hp Lycoming O-360 engine. (Donald Gray)

The drawing office at Beagle (Shoreham). (Donald Gray)

Shoreham airfield in the early 1960s. (Donald Gray)

Shoreham airfield in the late 1960s. (Donald Gray)

The cockpit of the Beagle B.206. (Donald Gray)

Manchester (Ringway) on 29 April 1957, killing the pilot and two passengers, and then on 17 December, an Aerovan (G-AJKP) crashed at Whiteheath, near Oldbury, Worcestershire, killing the pilot, Jean Lennox Bird (the first woman to receive RAF wings), and one passenger. The company later operated Miles Austers, an Avro Anson 19 II (G-AHKX) and an Airspeed Consul (G-AHEG).

By the end of the decade all of the British aircraft industry was in crisis, and many of the old and famous names were merged to form the British Aircraft Corporation. F. G. Miles Ltd was left to sort its own problems out, and so it was that the aircraft department became part of the new Beagle Company.

CHAPTER 6

1960–1969
The Beagle Has Landed

Since the end of the Second World War, the British aircraft industry had failed to produce light aircraft for major world markets, and over the last four years, a flood of foreign-built machines, the majority American, had been imported by British customers.

That was set to change when the British car body manufacturer Pressed Steel Company Ltd was persuaded by Sir Peter Masefield to invest in light aircraft, and subsequently took over the aviation interests of F. G. Miles Ltd and Auster Aircraft Ltd, of Rearsby, to form British Executive & General Aviation Ltd (Beagle Aircraft Ltd), at Shoreham, on 7 October 1960. George Miles was the chief designer and technical director of the company, which had initially been registered as Beagle-Miles Ltd, and the three parts of the company operated independently until they were merged at Shoreham in 1962.

The first British light aircraft that showed competitive promise over other rivals was the Beagle M.218, a four-seat twin-engined light, with an airframe of glass-fibre construction and extensive use of plastics. In 1960, Miles had roughed out three designs for the Kendall sailplane (although it was never used) but the testing carried out at the Royal Aircraft Establishment (RAE) produced details of where plastics could be used to reduce the complexity and costs of the airframe. Within weeks of setting up at Shoreham, design drawings were started for a new prototype twin-engine light transport aircraft, the Beagle B206X.

The summer of 1960 saw a marked increase in club and competition flying; the Shoreham Tournament took place over the weekend of 20–21 May 1960, and was made up of a series of tests. Day One was a distance event over a 380-mile course that started and ended at Shoreham, with turning points at Lympne, Sywell and Filton. Day Two comprised short take-offs, where contestants were required to clear a 10-foot barrier without dropping on to the ground after passing over it, and short-landing performances. In the third test the aircraft had to be parked on

'Modern Alarms' De Havilland Dove G-ALBM in the process of being scrapped at Shoreham on 5 May 1975. (Rob Finch)

a given position with the doors and hoods closed, the engine off, the petrol off and the aircraft chocked. On the start signal, the pilot had to run from the wing tip, enter the aircraft and start the engine. The time was noted from start to engine-running, and following this engine-starting test, the pilot had to negotiate his aircraft along a marked taxiway leading to a parking bay where the machine had to be stopped astride a marked centre line. This test of manoeuvrability was followed by a widely interpreted *Concours d'Élégance*, in which the aircraft was judged on (a) comfort and convenience for pilot and passengers; (b) general condition and flight operating equipment fitted; and (c) luggage allowance per passenger. During all these tests the aircraft were flown solo, and with full fuel tanks.

The aircraft types entered for the weekend included a DH Moth Minor (G-AFPN), a Rollason Turbulent (G-AJCP), Taylorcraft Plus-D (G-AHGZ), a Miles Gemini 3A (G-AKHC), a Garland Linnet (G-APNS), a Cessna 150 (G-APZR), 175 (G-APYA), and 210 (N7303E), a Piper Caribbean and TriPacer (G-APXM), and various Proctors, Chipmunks. The winners in the three categories received respectively the John Percival Challenge Cup, the Kemsley Challenge Trophy and the Grosvenor Challenge Cup. The class winner with the highest number of total points was declared the overall winner and received the Osram Cup, and cash prizes

RAF Westland Wessex HCC.2, XV732, of the Queen's Flight basks in the evening sunshine at Shoreham on 3 June 1974. (Rob Finch)

of £100, £75, £50 and £25 were awarded to the highest-placed entrants in each class. Two special prizes, of £50 and £25, were awarded for the best performance in aircraft registered before 1 January 1950.

A week later, the Royal Aero Club's Business and Touring Aircraft Competition was held at Shoreham. For a 5s entrance fee, the public were able to watch the day's spectacle, which began with the short-field testing of competing pilots for take-offs, in which they had to declare beforehand the distance in which they thought they could clear a line strung 10 feet high between two poles, and then back their verbal judgement with a run at full fuel load. The flying order was decided by ballot, and the aircraft were lined up two at a time. No practice had been possible due to poor weather conditions in the week leading up to the event. Nevertheless, some of the declared distances appeared to be impossibly close: 75 yards for a Super Cub, another of 100 yards for a Lancashire Aircraft EP-9 Prospector, and 130 yds for a Thruxton Jackaroo. The larger of the two Jodels – the D.140 Mousquetaire – had been declared to have a take-off distance 20 yards less than its smaller brother, the D.117, and, at 150 yards, made it safely. The most spectacular take-off in Class 1 was that of the Piper Super Cub, the Vigors Aviation entry for that class. From 75 yards, the 150-hp Cub simply leapt into the air, its tailwheel dragging, and cleared the 10-foot line at a quite extraordinary angle. Several competitors failed to make the 'jump', and hit the tape, which disqualified them.

A visiting RAF Hunting-Percival Pembroke about to go alongside a Haywards Aviation De Havilland Dove parked on the grass at Shoreham sometime in the mid-1970s. (Rob Finch)

The event was followed by a short-landing contest. This test was one of pure flying skill, and the general standard was high. Marks were deducted from 300 at the rate of one for each 2 yards of landing run, so that not only accurate judgement but a low landing speed and good brakes were a prerequisite of a good score, though many pilots complained that their aircraft were skidding on the grass. Wing Commander T. C. Murray in a Super Cub was the overall winner, with a declared take-off of 75 yards, and a landing of just 57 yards, scores which were considerably shorter than those of the other entrants of both classes.

Customs facilities were made available at Shoreham airport in September 1960, and in October, Miles Electronics Ltd were promoting their flight simulator, which had been ordered by the British Government for use by the Royal Navy and the Royal Air Force to assist in the training of aircrews.

In November, East Anglian Flying Services of Southend-on-Sea were granted their application by the Air Transport Licensing Board to operate vehicle ferries, and in accordance with demand, initially used Bristol 170s, with plans to gradually phase in the Aviation Traders ATL-98 Carvair for all of their scheduled services, including the Ipswich–Southend–Rochester–Shoreham–Alderney–Guernsey and Jersey route, and the Ipswich–Paris service via Southend–Rochester and Shoreham.

The Beagle B.206X (G-ARRM), built at Beagle's Rearsby factory near Leicester, was completed at Shoreham and first flown, to the acclaim of the aeronautical press, by John Nicolson on 15 August 1961. However, by 1963, internal disputes within the company led several of the senior staff to resign, or be dismissed, among them F. G. Miles himself. Shortly afterwards, his brother George also resigned, feeling that too little was being done to market his M.218, and following the rejection of an order for twenty aircraft from Germany.

The hopes for the company then hinged on the success of selling the B.206, later named the Bassett, to the RAF, who wanted to use them in their communications squadrons alongside De Havilland Devons, Hawker-Siddeley Andovers, and Bristol Sycamore helicopters. Around twenty Bassetts were initially delivered from an order of 250, but several failings were discovered when they were used in service; poor reliability, insufficient payload and range to transport V-bomber crews, problems with the undercarriage, and engine-related issues with the sump, the exhaust augmenter tubes, and engine bearer vibration led to the order for the aircraft being cut to just fifty. By May 1974, they would be withdrawn from service.

Beagle were also working with retired Wing Commander Kenneth Wallis, who had been experimenting on a two-seat autogyro, based on the Benson gyrocopter, the Wallis WA-116, which had its first flight on 2 August 1961. This small venture saw five being ordered for evaluation by the Army, and three being used as *Little*

Arriving from Rome, Italy, en-route to the Farnborough International Airshow, is the Maritime Patrol & Rescue Tri-turbo 3 *Spirit of Hope* (N23SA) on the apron at Shoreham on 2 September 1978. (Rob Finch)

Nellie (G-ARZB) in the 1967 James Bond film *You Only Live Twice*, piloted for the footage by Wallis himself.

J. W. Charles 'Pee-wee' Judge, an ex-RAF Spitfire and Typhoon pilot who had recently been a test pilot on the Tyne-Ambassador and Conway-Vulcan programmes of Rolls-Royce Ltd, joined Beagle at Shoreham in 1961. He was appointed as Chief Test Pilot of the Beagle Group in 1962, and during his eight years of strenuous work at Shoreham and Rearsby, he made the first flights of twelve different types of Beagle light aircraft – from the B.206Y prototype on 12 August 1962 to the Bulldog prototype on 19 May 1969. Judge was killed in a flying accident at the SBAC (Society of British Aerospace Companies) show at Farnborough on 11 September 1970.

In 1964, South Coast Air Taxis requested a 1,500-yard east–west runway suitable for Bristol Freighters and Short Skyvans, but local opposition led to public enquiries being held, and the application was ultimately rejected, though it was considered a suitable possibility for the future. The airfield, being just 6 feet above sea level, quickly became waterlogged, and in continuous wet weather could not drain fast enough to take off and land with the regularity necessary to provide the airport with a steady income.

United Arab Emirates Air Force De Havilland (Canada) DHC-5 Buffalo serial '309' on delivery through Shoreham on 30 August 1979. (Rob Finch)

A tragic accident occurred in the afternoon of 13 March in which a young pilot, Colin Barrett, and his passenger, Mr Ginn, were both killed shortly after take-off from Shoreham in a De Havilland DH-82 Tiger Moth (G-AKXO) of the Southern Aero Club. The aircraft was seen to go into a spin, and crashed in the front garden of 77 Buckingham Road, which was unoccupied at the time. Cecil Pashley, CFI at the club, stated that he had flown the aircraft earlier in the day, and there were no faults with it.

A second fatal accident at Shoreham occurred just two months later, on 25 May, when the second prototype Beagle B.206Y (G-ARXM) crashed at Wisborough Green, near Horsham, killing the company pilot Ralph Spackman, who was returning to Shoreham after giving a demonstration at Wisley.

January 1965 was marked by another fatal accident on the 5th, when a Bölkow 107c (G-ASAW) crashed into the sea while performing acrobatics. Remnants showed that the aircraft had struck the water at a speed higher than that which would have been normal for intentional ditching. The pilot was Donald Jarvis, CFI at Sussex Flying Training Facilities, and his pupil, Peter Philips, was also on board.

On 12 June 1965, the first qualifying round of the National Air Races organised by the Royal Aero Club was held at Shoreham for the John Morgan Challenge Trophy (the second race was to be held at Middleton St George on 7 August, and

Beagle B.206S G-AWRM at the fuel pumps at Shoreham airport in January 1979. (Rob Finch)

the twenty-four entrants with the highest number of points from the combined total of both races went forward to the Kings Cup at Coventry on 24 August). The course differed that year by having the finishing line off Worthing pier instead of Brighton Pier, thus shortening it by 13 miles to 87 miles. From Shoreham airport, and round a scatter point on Shoreham beach, the circuit went via Beachy Head lighthouse to the Martello tower on Langney Point, then a small pylon on the private landing strip at Deanland Farm, near Hailsham, to Knepp Castle, an ancient monument 5 miles south of Horsham, then the control tower at the disused Ford naval air station, on to the end of the jetty at Littlehampton, and finally along an 8-mile leg to the finishing line off Worthing pier.

Practice on the Friday afternoon was badly disorganised by sea fog, the old South Coast bugbear. It drifted in, and in a matter of minutes blanketed the coast, the airfield and part of the course, with the result that aircraft already in the air were forced to land at airfields over a wide area from Blackbushe to Deanland Farm. Early on the Saturday morning, to anyone not knowing about the chaos of the evening before, the race looked like it would be badly supported, with the possibility of no race at all. However, as the morning wore on the aircraft returned and the pilots reported in and departed once again for another try at the course.

The third and last race of the afternoon was strictly 'ladies only' – believed to be the first of its kind, other than informal contests, ever held in this country. The organisers were the British section of the 'American 99s Association', and the first prize was a challenge trophy presented by the Champion Sparking Plug Company.

The sea fog forecast for 6 p.m. fortunately failed to materialise, and the nine contestants duly took off in handicapped order. Sheila Scott in her Comanche 250 soon overhauled the majority of the slower aircraft, and on the final leg passed the leading machine up to that time, the British Women Pilots' Association's Condor, piloted by Christine Hughes of *Flight*, to win by twenty-four seconds; ex-ATA pilot Diana Barnato Walker, who, on 26 August 1963, flew an English Electric Lightning, attaining 1,262 mph (Mach 1.65), and became the first British woman to exceed the speed of sound, came third in the Auster Alpine of the Girls Venture Corps Air Wing.

Cecil Pashley, MBE (1948), who had set up the Shoreham Flying Club in 1911 and had logged over 20,000 flying hours, mostly as an instructor, had to seriously contemplate retiring after the Ministry of Aviation refused to renew his licence. He was seventy-four years old at the time, but he won an appeal against the decision, and had his licence restored under the condition that he always flew accompanied by another licensed pilot. Pashley passed away on 10 December 1969, survived by his wife Vera, who had supported him over a career that spanned over sixty years.

An Empire Test Pilot School Hawker-Siddeley Andover C.1 (XS606), seen at Shoreham in August 1981 during their annual visit to Singer Link-Miles at nearby Lancing. (Rob Finch)

A portrait of 'Pash', painted by his daughter Nonie, was presented to the Southern Aero Club, and the eastern perimeter road was officially named *Cecil Pashley Way* in his honour.

Beagle Aircraft Ltd was nationalised in late 1966 and taken over by the British Motor Corporation, but the aviation aspects were not required, and Fred Mulley, the then Minister of Aviation, announced that the Government would buy Beagle for £1 million; the alternative was a complete shutdown with around a thousand redundancies.

The prototype of the Beagle B.121 Pup (G-AVDF) made its first flight on 8 April 1967, flown by 'Pee-wee' Judge, and the first customer for it was the Shoreham School of Flying. Having four Pup-100s and a Pup-150, a contract for twelve more initiated the dealership for their associated company, Shoreham Aviation Services. However, the Pups and a Beagle B.206 were disposed of by the flying club in September in a part-exchange deal for five Cessnas – three 150s, a 172 and a 337. Peter Hewitt, managing director of the school, claimed that he had a number of problems with his Pups and that he had received inadequate cooperation from Beagle Aircraft, though individual company staff had been helpful. Brakes and shock absorbers on the aircraft had required frequent replacement, and on one occasion, a fuel tank in the 150 split while the aircraft was airborne.

Some of the problems seemed to concern both the Series 100 aircraft, which were among the first Pups to come off the Beagle production line, and the Series 150 (the sixty-second to be produced) delivered on 27 June 1969. Beagle's decision to increase the club landing fees at Shoreham – hitherto a 'goodwill' charge of only 10s a week to 2s 6d per 1,000 lbs had apparently influenced the decision to part-exchange the aircraft.

Beagle claimed that initial teething troubles with the aircraft had been few, and limited to specific areas, and that the first batch of production Pups had been as good as, or better than, any overseas design at a similar stage. Hard flying-club use had shown that certain improvements were possible and desirable, and successful redesign action on these areas had been completed.

Mr K. N. Myer was the new managing director at Beagle, and brought his industrialist and specialist experience in production and export to the fore, transforming the organisation of the company to realise the tremendous potential of the Pup and to make Beagle into a healthy, expanding business with a profitable long-term future. Under his charge, the Pup proved to be very successful, sold in great numbers, and looked to provide the turning point for the fortunes of the company. With the fuselages, final assembly and flight testing being done at Shoreham, and the factory in Rearsby making the wings and tailplanes, it was

Lancashire/Edgar Percival EP.9 Prospector G-APWZ at Shoreham airport in summer 1982. (Rob Finch)

expected in due course that the entire production would be concentrated in the fully developed Shoreham factory, with hopes of its worldwide military sales potential.

However, sales for Beagle 206s to the Argentine Air Force were dashed in 1968 when the whole affair was thrown into suspense by the British embargo on Argentine meat imports following the outbreak of foot-and-mouth disease, and their design of the M100 Student jet-trainer, which was aimed at the military market, had failed to win a government contract. While the B.125 Bulldog was being developed from the Pup, the company, asking the Government for more financial help, was instead put into receivership.

The receiver tried to revive and sell the company (now renamed Beagle Aircraft (1969) Ltd), but failed, and the company assets were disposed of. Scottish Aviation of Prestwick took over the export orders and the RAF contract for the Bulldog, of which 326 were built.

After the split from Beagle, the Miles brothers had set up Miles Engineering, which built replica aircraft (one of these being a 1910 Bristol Boxkite (G-ASPP) which was used as *The Phoenix Flyer* and inaccurately referred to as a Curtiss in the 1965 film *Those Magnificent Men in their Flying Machines*), and Miles-Dufon

British Airways Sikorsky H.34T G-BCLO seen crew training down at Shoreham back in the 1980s. (Rob Finch)

Ltd, subcontractors for the Short Brothers 'Skyvan' series, which were designed as regional airliners.

Beagle, who would provide other airport facilities, including air traffic control, also offered the nostalgically named Miles Hawk trainer (the Miles M.2 Hawk aircraft was built in 1933 at Woodley aerodrome) as one of their packages for the civil market by their electronics division. The basic trainer could be representative of any jet aircraft, its approximate weight being determined by settings in the computer. Each trainer flight deck had one throttle lever and one engine instrument (usually percentage thrust), an undercarriage lever and a flap lever. Asymmetric characteristics could be built in, but at a price, which varied between £25,000 and £150,000 depending on the customer requirements.

In view of the proposed work that was expected to be undertaken in 1968 on the construction of an (03/21) asphalt runway at Shoreham, for a proposed opening date of May 1969, an order was submitted by the urban district council of Shoreham-on-Sea to divert the course of a public footpath that ran from a point west of the gate by the south-west corner of the aerodrome, north-westerly to Mossy Bottom Farm, Old Shoreham. The application was rejected, the belief from the opposition being that it would result in the arrival of heavier and noisier

Agusta-Bell 206B Jet Ranger II G-FSDG at Shoreham in 1986. (Neil Randell)

aircraft, but it was advised that a north-east–south-west runway would be the most suitable possibility.

During a display by the Tiger Club on 11 August 1968, a balloon-busting show went tragically wrong when one of the balloons got caught up in the wing of a Druine D.31 Turbulent (G-ASDB), causing it to crash, killing the pilot.

In a report to the joint owners of the airfield, Peter Masefield, chairman of the British Airports Authority, said,

> General aviation at Gatwick, mostly business aircraft, is increasing by more than 30 per cent per annum. All the indications are that Gatwick will reach its capacity by about the summer of 1974 and that business flying, ideally suited to Shoreham, will have to be hived off ahead of that date.

On 1 January 1969, the Airways Group of companies, based at Gatwick Airport, and comprising Air London Ltd, Airways Training Ltd, and Airways Brokers (Sales) Ltd, bought a ⅔ share in the Shoreham Aviation Group of companies. The latter included the Shoreham School of Flying (four Beagle Pups, two Bölkow Juniors and

De Havilland DH-104 Devon C2 G-DEVN (now preserved in Merseburg, Germany), seen here at Shoreham in 1986. (Neil Randell)

Air UK Handley Page Herald G-APWF overshooting Shoreham during the 1980 airshow. (Rob Finch)

one Cherokee used on pilot training), Shoreham Aviation Ltd (charter company using one Beagle B.206 and one Piper Twin Comanche), and Shoreham Aviation Services (Maintenance Engineering Company). The shares were acquired from two of the three former holders of the Shoreham group – from George Lowdell and A. J. Falwasser. The holding of Frank Hewitt was unchanged – his wholly owned Hewitt Investment Company owned the Beagle Pups and the two light twins that were leased to the operating companies.

The day was marred by news of the death of the British aviation pioneer Cecil Pashley, MBE, AFC, who was seventy-eight years old.

CHAPTER 7

1970–1989
The Way Ahead Part 1

Following the recession that had hit the general aviation industry by the late 1960s, the signs of recovery were slow to appear, and this was evident at Shoreham. In February 1970, following the sad demise of Beagle Aircraft Ltd (which was the main theme of a Commons debate on 27 January), the tenancy of the airfield was handed back to the Joint Municipal Airport Committee, and by June, a public enquiry was still in progress about planning permission for a concrete runway. Final contracts were also being drawn up for the sale of the ex-Beagle facilities at Shoreham airport to Miles Aviation and Transport, based at Ford aerodrome. Miles would also take over the running of Shoreham airport under a lease from the Brighton, Hove and Worthing Joint Committee.

Toon Ghose joined Cecil Pashley at the Southern Aero Club as its CFI in 1968. Ghose, who was born in India, had had a fascination with planes and flying since the age of six, where he first saw a Tiger Moth displaying at an air show, and left Calcutta in 1955 to go to France (riding all the way on a Vespa motor scooter), where he learnt to glide. He set an Indian gliding record by flying up to 25,000 feet. After then learning to fly powered aircraft, he moved to England, where he obtained his commercial pilot's licence. During the 1970s, he set up his own business, Toon Ghose Aviation Ltd, after taking over the Brighton Flying Group, and operated a De Havilland Chipmunk 'Lillibet', and two Cessna 152s.

An accident in the early evening of 10 October 1978 resulted in the deaths of two pilots, one from Dan Air and the other from British Airtours, when they were performing stall turns in one of the company's Cessnas (G-TOON), but at the end of one manoeuvre they were unable to pull up in time and crashed into the sea. Toon's company continued until the credit squeeze of the 1980s caused many businesses to go into voluntary liquidation, and sadly, his became one of them in 1983.

In March 1971, Shoreham School of Flying had completed arrangements with Deauville Flying Club for a mutual programme of flying and social events, which would open with a weekend visit by Deauville pilots in May, to be reciprocated by Shoreham in June or July, with competitive events to be held throughout the year.

Arrangements were also under way between Douglas Bunn, proprietor of the Southern Aero Club, and Peter Hewitt, managing director of the Shoreham School of Flying, towards an amalgamation of the two clubs, and it was hoped that the merger would see improved facilities for both private and charter flying. The clubs had adjoining premises at Shoreham airport and a total membership of about 900, and combined operations under the control of Hewitt began nominally on 1 May, in the name of the Shoreham School of Flying, which had recently taken delivery of a Britten-Norman BN-2A Islander (G-AXXJ).

On 15 May 1971, Shoreham reverted to its status as a municipal airport, with Alexander Ewan 'Ben' Gunn, MBE, as manager. Passenger services and general aviation became the focus of attention, but even then, there were some doubts about its future. There was no absolute shortage of airfields in the south-east of England and those that existed were not necessarily in the best places for their users or for the environment. Shoreham, being prone to water logging, and having seen the collapse of some of the tenant companies, held limited attraction for potential businesses or investors. One person who did invest, however, was Roy Spooner, who set up Spooner Aviation with big spares backing and factory-trained engineers in a new, modern sales centre. As the British agent for Enstrom Helicopters, and in particular the F-28A, the company had made twenty-three deliveries in the UK, with more on order by the middle of 1974.

Shoreham Aviation started offering a full range of light charter services with an Islander aircraft in November, after being granted an Air Operator's Certificate.

The Shoreham School of Flying was bought by Lonmet (Aviation) Ltd in April 1972, and was the last in a series of acquisitions by the company. The new owners had no immediate plans for changing the school but intended to start instrument and twin training. Lonmet chairman R. J. Pascoe reported that this latest purchase completed his plans for expansion in the current year. The group, which began with Southend Aero Club, also owned Ipswich Airfield, the East Anglia Flying Club, and Flairavia and Delta Aircraft Sales of Biggin Hill, and had a total fleet of twenty-two aircraft.

Several flying schools were running concurrently at this time, and as one business failed, another would start up; at one stage there were eight fixed wing schools as well as helicopter training schools. This didn't put off airline pilot John Pothecary and his wife Jenny, a former hostess for British United Airways, and a qualified flying instructor, setting up their own flying training business, Air South Ltd, in the former drawing office of F. G. Miles Ltd. With John's main income dependent on his job with Air UK, Jenny took over the running of the club as well as an engineering section, which catered for both vintage and current types of aircraft. The company was sold to Southern Air Ltd in 1996.

The tide was to turn again for the fortunes of the airport when JFA (John Fisher Airlines) began scheduled services between Shoreham and the Channel Islands on 2 May 1972. The airline was formed at Portsmouth in 1971, using a Twin Pioneer, and 7,800 passengers were carried between the Channel Isles and the mainland. The company, under its new name Jersey Ferry Airlines, expected to move more than 25,000 passengers in its first year.

The *Daily Express* Air Race, run in conjunction with the Biggin Hill Air Fair, took place on 19–20 May, with Shoreham being the start and finish points for the rally. A twenty-four-hour separation was provided to give more time for handicapping the first fifty aircraft in the rally.

Miles-Dufon was the English dealer for the North American Rockwell (NAR) Turbo Commander 690. John Doyle, NAR's representative in Geneva, took a demonstration 690 to Shoreham, where it was shown to customers and the press. This aircraft had an unusual background in that, even before it had been publicly announced, the first production aircraft had crossed the Atlantic and been subjected to a comprehensive evaluation by the Ministry of Defence (Procurement Executive) at its Boscombe Down flight-test centre.

Shoreham was listed, along with with Denham, Biggin Hill and Kidlington, as having shown a notable growth rate in a study of general aviation conducted in 1973, for the Standing Conference on London and South East Regional Planning. The study, which considered forty-five airfields (twenty of which had at least one hard runway but were let down by their hangarage) in an area bounded by Luton and Stansted to the north, Kidlington to the west and Shoreham to the south, was produced in response to local authorities who had indicated a need for the small airfields in their regions to be considered in their local and regional plans.

In April 1973, F .G. Miles Engineering Ltd won a contract to develop a new light stores carrier for helicopters and fixed-wing aircraft under the British Ministry of Defence Procurement Executive. The eighteen-month project combined the company's work on free-fall release units with a crutchless suspension system developed by RAE Farnborough. Stores weighing up to 50 lb would be carried by the new equipment. The company also won a contract to supply Messerschmitt-Bölkow-Blohm (Munich) with MAL 19 actuators to be incorporated in the heavy-duty ejector release units being developed for Multi-Role Combat Aircraft.

It was announced in September that full Customs facilities would shortly be introduced at the airport after an interim period, when they would be available on a concessional basis at two hours' notice. As well as benefiting business aviation and private flying, the move would allow Jersey Ferry Airlines to operate very keenly-priced (£15.30 for a return) direct flights to the Channel Islands instead of via Portsmouth, where, until then, customs had to be cleared. The airline's winter schedules showed two weekly Trislander flights to both Jersey and Guernsey.

A further encouraging sign for Shoreham airport was its development as a light aviation centre. Miles-Dufon and Spooner Aviation were joined by Rollason Aircraft and Engines and also by Phoenix Aircraft, and it was hoped that light aircraft would again be built at Shoreham and that they would meet with more success than some of the machines that had been made there in the past.

The Calloway Shield, a trophy awarded for the efficiency of airfield fire and rescue crews, was won for the second year in succession in March 1974 by Shoreham airport. Snap checks were made at various times during the year and a simulated crash arranged to test the crews' reaction time and effectiveness.

Further good news announced for the airfield was that the installation of new drains had largely eliminated the flooding problems which in the past had beset the field. Shoreham airport is below the high-tide level of the River Adur, from which it is separated by a single embankment.

Intra Airways Ltd, a private British independent airline, began a scheduled passenger service in 1974 with their Douglas DC-3s, operating thirty weekly flights between Shoreham airport and Jersey and/or Guernsey, with an extension to Gatwick.

In October 1976, the management at Shoreham invited operators who were deterred from using Gatwick by recently imposed constraints on general aviation to 'come on in', boasting that it would reduce their costs with its lower landing fees, no requirement for handling agents, and a 'readily' available customs service (overnight notice was necessary); it would also speed up their turnround time.

Shoreham was being used by some 200 businesses by 1977. An aeronautical college had been established, and despite the lack of a hard runway, charter flights and air taxis operated on the 03/21. The 03 runway was most practical because the Lancing gap worked wonders; it effectively shoved the wind round to the north, and with about 1,000 yards available, the hedge speed could be kept on the generous side.

Haywards Aviation, which later merged with Jersey European Airways, began operating services using Piper Aztecs in 1977, and Aurigny Air Services, which advertised itself as 'The Channel Islands' Own Airline' and was the first commercial operator of the Britten-Norman Trislander (and the first airline in the world to ban smoking on all services), set up at Shoreham in the following year, offering services to Alderney from 1979.

A privately owned Jodel DR.1050 Ambassadeur (G-AVIU) crashed and burnt out on Sandown golf course during a flight from Shoreham to the Isle of Wight on 14 June, killing both the pilot, Anthony Roads, and its owner, Peter Cremer. There is confusion over the date of the crash; 1 August 1986 has been suggested, but the registration of the aircraft was cancelled by the UK Civil Aviation Authority on 6 August 1986.

British Caledonian Helicopters, which was formed when it took over Ferranti Helicopters in April 1979, set up in the hangar and ex-home of the Beagle aircraft, and in 1980 started operating ad hoc charter, air-taxi and lighthouse support work with Bell 206s, Bölkow 105s and a half-dozen additional aircraft.

As a base for 140 aircraft, used by 280 different business aircraft a year, and with scheduled services running daily to the Channel Islands and Dieppe, Shoreham airport needed a tarmac strip. There was a third public enquiry in 1980, this time with the backing of Michael Heseltine, who at the time was Secretary of State for Defence, and who supported the creation of a hard runway. He allocated £250,000 for its construction with the understanding that it would have a maximum length of 830 yards, that it would only be used between 7 a.m. and 9 p.m., and that there were not to be more than 75,000 movements a year.

A Fournier RF-4D owned by John Cromwell-Morgan crash-landed by the A27 shortly after take-off from Shoreham on 12 January 1981. The aircraft was on its initial climb, and an eyewitness said it was too 'tail-down', giving the impression that the engine was losing power. Mr Cromwell-Morgan died in hospital three months later.

A 5-foot-long unexploded German bomb was discovered 8 feet in the ground just north of the main runway in February 1982. It still bore the unmistakable stamp of an eagle – the symbol of the Third Reich – when ten men from the Army bomb-disposal team lifted it out of its crater, and, after drilling two holes in its side, then worked for six hours to pump the explosive out with steam before being satisfied that it was safe and giving the 'all clear' at 1 a.m. the following morning. The defused bomb was later placed on show in the terminal building. Army chiefs warned that the airfield could be riddled with similar unexploded bombs.

Work was begun on the long-awaited tarmac runway on 12 October by S. M. Tidy (Public Works) Ltd, of Brighton, and it was completed in June 1982, with an official opening on 18 September. Ben Gunn, who had been airport manager for the last twelve years, was delighted. Vital business flights had to be cancelled each time heavy rain fell and flooded the grass airfield, and many pilots were reluctant to use Shoreham because of the condition of the landing strip, and would often have to divert to Southampton, to the great inconvenience of the passengers. The occasion was marked with a visit to the airport by Airship Industries' 150-foot Skyship 500 (G-BIHN), which would later be used in the 1985 James Bond film *A View to a Kill*.

Jersey European Airways was rapidly developing its services in 1983 after a rise of nearly 60 per cent from the previous year, and were considering adding two Fokker F.27s to its fleet. The carrier currently flew from Guernsey to Shoreham and Stansted; from Stansted to Brussels; from Dinard to Shoreham and Gatwick; and from Liverpool to Dublin. However, the company, failing to make a profit, discontinued their services and closed in 1986; the company was taken over by South-East Air (of Biggin Hill) until their own collapse in 1988.

Keith Wickenden, the Conservative MP for Dorking (1979–83), and the chairman of European Ferries, had a replacement engine fitted to his De Havilland DH-104 Dove 2A (G-AMYP), and afterwards took off from Shoreham for a short test flight to check the engine. Just after rotation, the engine was heard to splutter, and the aircraft was unable to maintain height due to suspected right engine failure. It dived into the bank of the River Adur and exploded, killing Mr Wickenden.

In 1984, the terminal building was designated Grade II listed for the principal reasons that it was an unusual survivor from the early days of civil aviation

Against the background of the imposing structure of the Lancing College Chapel, an ex-RAF De Havilland (Canada) DHC.1 Chipmunk performs a spirited display at the RAFA Airshow at Shoreham on 30 August 1997. (Rob Finch)

transport, and its landscape setting, with adjacent original airfield and hangar, made it particularly rare and of more than special interest. This type of survival was very rare for a working airport, and, despite some later changes made to the original plan (both internal and external), was still intact.

The building has been used to film scenes set in Singapore for the BBC series *Tenko*. It was also used in the series *Fortunes of War* (1987); three episodes of the David Suchet series *Poirot*, 'The Adventure of the Western Star' (1990), 'Death in the Clouds' (1992), and 'Lord Edgware Dies' (2000); and in 2005 it was 'transformed' into Le Bourget airport in France for the Tom Hanks film *The Da Vinci Code*. The most recent use was in the controversial feature-length documentary *Angel without Wings* in 2011.

Shoreham played host to 'General Aviation-USA-84', a show sponsored by the US Department of Commerce to launch an American bid to expand sales of its business aircraft and equipment in the UK and Europe. The show ran from 4 to 6 June 1984, and exhibitors at the event (attended by invitation) were eligible only if their products were 'fifty per cent or more American-made by hardware', if they were seeking US partners for joint UK/US manufacturing, or if they were developing European marketing projects for US general aviation aircraft, avionics, or systems. With its tarmac runway supplementing its three grass runways, the invited delegates were welcomed to fly to the show, although no demonstration flying was permitted over the field.

CHAPTER 8

1985–2005
The Way Ahead Part II

A Rheims Cessna 172N Skyhawk II (G-BFOW) took off from Shoreham en route to Jersey on 10 February 1985, and the former Dan Air pilot, David Regi, sent out a 'mayday' distress call with the information that the aircraft would not be able to make Alderney; the engine had cut out, or was cutting out, and, at a range of about 13 miles north-west of Alderney, would be ditching in the next two to three minutes. The aircraft was not seen again. A full air and sea search was initiated, but nothing was found. Wreckage from the aircraft was recovered 12 miles south of Swanage, Dorset, just over a year later, but the reason for the disappearance of the aircraft is still shrouded in mystery.

The Kings Cup Air Race was held on 15–16 September 1985, the first time it had been staged at Shoreham since 1936, and the event now included foreign-built aircraft. It was won by Gordon Franks in a SIAI-Marchetti SF.260 (G-BDEN), and he received the much-coveted trophy from Prince Andrew at the Royal Aero Club awards ceremony some weeks later at the RAF Museum, Hendon. The race itself, however, saw twenty-three of the twenty-six entrants disqualified for cutting corners or flying too low, and one failed to finish.

In 1986, a new taxiway from the airport apron was laid to enable three-way operation, and the profile of the air traffic control tower was altered with a small extension to the south of the original control room, and an observation room (a small glass-enclosed structure on the top of the control tower) was built (this was replaced in 1987 by an all-glass observation room, following storm damage).

In the worst storm since 1 January 1949, when a 'miniature whirlwind' left a trail of destruction from Worthing to Shoreham, and caused a double-decker bus with twenty-five people on board to be blown off the Old Shoreham Bridge and into the Adur, twenty-seven aircraft were damaged at Shoreham airport in the early hours of 16 October 1987. Of these, fourteen were damaged by falling debris in a hangar, and outside, a Cessna F172N Skyhawk (G-BGNS) owned by Reedtrend Ltd, and

Sussex Police MD-902 Explorer G-SUSX at Shoreham on 14 September 2008. (Neil Randell)

A Harrier of 41 Squadron, ZG-503, sits in the static park for the 2009 airshow. (Rob Finch)

A Vampire T-11 (WZ507, also G-VTII based at Bournemouth) at the Shoreham Airshow in August 2008. (Nick Denbow)

The only airworthy Avro Vulcan, XH588, at the Shoreham Airshow in August 2009. (Nick Denbow)

Resident MD902 Explorer G-SUSX of Sussex Police at Shoreham on 14 March 2010. (Neil Randell)

Robinson R.22 Beta G-OKEY on the Fast Helicopters apron at Shoreham on 14 March 2010. (Neil Randell)

a Cessna 152 (G-BGHA) of Stanton Aircraft Management Ltd were flipped and blown together; both were subsequently written off. A maximum gust of 115 mph had been recorded at Shoreham-by-Sea.

Shoreham's famous annual air show was founded and run by the Royal Air Forces Association (RAFA) in August 1989, and has continued to be one of the most enjoyable and well-rounded air displays of the year. What had started as a small fête in a corner of the airfield away from the day-to-day operations now boasts a wide variety of ground displays by the local flying clubs, the armed forces, classic car and vehicle clubs, as well as funfairs, craft markets, simulators and rides, is now one of the most prodigious airshows in the country, and raising more money for the RAFA Wings Appeal, which raises money to provide welfare and comradeship to the RAF families, than any other branch in the country.

The airshow has many static displays and a flying programme that has included Vic Norman and his famous AeroSuperBatics team, who perform with their four Boeing-Stearman Model 75 biplanes with Sarah Tanner, Danielle Hughes and Stella Guilding as the *Breitling Wing Walkers* (they have supported the airshow from its

Army Chipmunk WP298 in front of the fuel store and bowsers on 14 September 2008. (Neil Randell)

Cessna T303 Crusader G-CMOS at Shoreham on 14 March 2010. (Neil Randell)

Christen Eagle II G-OEGL at Shoreham on 14 March 2010. (Neil Randell)

first year, and have previously flown – according to their sponsors at the time – as *Team Guinot*, the *Utterly Butterly Wing-walking Display Team* and the *Crunchie Wing-walking Display Team*; the Blades (four ex-Red Arrows pilots) aerobatics team of four Extra 300LP aircraft; Paul Bonhomme and Steve Jones from the Red Bull Air Races with their close aerobatic formation as *The Matadors* in their Sukhoi SU-26 aircraft; the RAF Falcons Parachute Display Team; the Red Arrows; nine Hawker-Siddeley Gnats (these were replaced in 1979 with BAE Hawk T-1s), producing their trademark red, white and blue smoke; the Avro Vulcan (XH-588) - the only airworthy example of the 134 Avro Vulcan V bombers that were operated by the RAF from 1953 until 1984; the Eurofighter Typhoon; the Black Cats Royal Navy front-line Lynx maritime attack helicopter team; the Swift Aerobatic Glider Display Team; the Battle of Britain Memorial Flight; and jet aircraft such as the Danish F-16 Fighting Falcon, De Havilland Sea Vixen, and a host of vintage piston-engine, turbo-prop, and jet aircraft.

A Second World War airfield scramble, which has become a standard feature of the two-day event, enacts an attack by enemy planes represented by a Messerschmitt Bf-108 and a Hispano Aviacion HA-1112 MIL Buchon. Explosions, smoke and

Piper PA-31-350 Navajo G-OJIL of Redhill Charters at Shoreham on 14 March 2010. (Neil Randell)

Piper PA-28-180 Cherokee G-AVBT at Shoreham on 14 September 2008. (Neil Randell)

flames on the airfield create the effects of a real airborne attack before the good guys, Spitfires of various marks, close in for the attack and chase out the marauding enemy aircraft. Flypasts are performed by the Lancaster and escort of Spitfire and Hurricane of the Battle of Britain Memorial Flight (BBMF), and the Boeing B-17 *Sally B*. 212 Squadron (Living History Group) provide a full programme of ground displays that include drill parades and inspections, and set up a mock-up of a Battle of Britain Operations room with a compliment of WAAFs and senior officers, sentries, and pilots, all in full uniform and flying kit.

John Haffenden, who had been involved at the airport in various capacities throughout his working life, and was the last employee to be engaged by Cecil Pashley at the Southern Aero Club in 1968, gained his ATC licence in 1973, and became Senior Air Traffic Controller in 1990.

The Sussex Flying Club (Southern Aero Club's immediate successor) set up in an office situated on the first floor of the main terminal building in 1992, and, run by two of the former club's instructors, operated a fleet of Cessna and Piper aircraft. SkyLeisure Aviation (charters) was also established at the airport in 1992 under the ownership of David Chowen, while he was still flying for British Airways as a

A crowded main apron on 14 March 2010. (Neil Randell)

A busy flying day ahead on 14 March 2010. (Neil Randell)

The art deco terminal on 14 September 2009. (Neil Randell)

Boeing 737 captain. Redair Aviation Ltd took over the company in 1997, and on 5 January 1998, flying instructor Zahurul Islam and pilot Miss Jill Susan Develin were appointed as directors. Omega Sky Taxi Ltd t/a Omega Flight Training took over in June 2013 (initially trading with both names). Omega is an EASA/UK CAA Approved Training Organisation in its own right.

On 2 March 1996, pilot Malcolm Allen went to Clip Gate Farm, Canterbury, Kent, to pick up his new aircraft, a Jodel D9 Bebe (G-AXOI). The aircraft was checked thoroughly and after a twenty minute test flight, took off again at 1150 hrs for a flight to Shoreham airport.

On approach to runway 03, a Luton Minor (G-BBCY) had landed and was blocking the runway with a stopped engine, and 'OI' was told to go around, and report on final approach. The Luton Minor had been cleared off the runway, but the vehicle which had been sent to assist was still on the runway so 'OI' was told to go around again and the instruction was acknowledged. The frequency was then blocked for about twenty seconds by a helicopter requesting lift off, and when

Cessna 172M Skyhawk G-CDDK of Scenic Flights on the main apron on 14 September 2010. (Neil Randell)

A diesel-engined Diamond DA.42 Twin Star, G-JKMH, with the Sussex Pad and Lancing College on 17 October 2010. (Rob Finch)

Northbrook College workshops on 19 August 2009. (Clive Barker)

the transmission finished 'OI' called 'engine stop' followed by about four seconds of open microphone during which the sound of the engine, which could be heard quite clearly on previous transmissions, was not evident.

When it was over the field between houses and the railway embankment which crosses the undershoot to runway 03, 'OI' was seen to bank right and then steeply left, and then descend rapidly in the left turn and struck the ground in a steep nose down attitude. Several bystanders ran to give assistance, and within minutes the police helicopter, which is based at Shoreham, was at the site. The fuselage and wings were pulled clear so that the paramedic from the helicopter could gain better access. The pilot's harness was unfastened, but no signs of life were evident.

In 1998, the 03/21 runway was extended towards the south-west by 231 feet to accommodate heavy longer-range aircraft, and illuminated by omnidirectional low-intensity white edge lights (previously a flare path used to have to be laid out), and on its opening in April, a Dornier 328 (D-CHIC) landed to demonstrate the potential use of the 1,133-yard runway. In the following year, a parallel grass

On a cold and crisp winter's day in 2010, a snowman stands guard over the Sussex Flying Club line-up at Shoreham airport. (Rob Finch)

BAC 167 Strikemaster at the Shoreham Airshow on 21 August 2010. (Steven Whitehead)

Above and below: Harrier GR9 ZG858 at Shoreham Airshow, 21 August 2010. (Steven Whitehead)

landing strip was established alongside the hard runway, and a new taxiway was built from the apron in front of the tower via the holding points for runways 31 and 25, and on to the holding point for runway 21 to give a three-way option for operations. The grass runways are unlit, and the 02 approach (02/20) has a displaced threshold due to an elevated railway line along the southern aerodrome boundary.

From February 1999, a noise abatement procedure was in operation at Shoreham for runway 21. When given departure clearance for the west from this runway, the statement 'right turn after the coast' is always used, so that aircraft on full power climb are not overflying the built-up areas of Lancing and East Worthing.

The Phoenix Flying School was established in 1999 by Chief Flying Instructor, Examiner and Test Pilot Stuart McKinnon (who had been specialising in vintage, tailwheel and aerobatic flight training since 1996), with pilots Andy Reohorn, former motorcycle champion Justyn Gorman, Adrian Read, and James Hepnar, to meet the growing need for high-quality pilot training.

A helicopter left Shoreham on the morning of Saturday 18 September 1999, on a memorial flight to re-enact the first manned flight by Harold Piffard, which had taken place there in 1910. Following the original route and timing exactly, the pilot,

A dogfight ensues over Shoreham airfield between a Me 109 Hispano Buchon and a Spitfire on 21 August 2010. (Steven Whitehead)

A dogfight ensues over Shoreham airfield between a Me 109 Hispano Buchon and a Spitfire on 21 August 2010. (Steven Whitehead)

The air traffic control tower on 28 August 2010. (Adam Tinworth)

Ian MacGregor, finally landed at the Pad where he was met by the landlord, Wally Pack, who presented him with a gift of champagne. The event, which was organised by Tim Webb, co-author of the book *Shoreham Airport, Sussex* (second edition, 1999); Janet Pennington, college archivist; and Sylvia Adams, aviation historian; and attended by airport staff and other interested parties, is commemorated by a framed memorial, which was unveiled in the Sussex Pad by Ian Elliott, resident of Shoreham and chairman of West Sussex County Council. Wally Pack kindly agreed to ensure its future care.

Shoreham airport entered the new millennium as a busy, thriving general aviation airport with full air traffic control, three grass runways, and a full tarmac runway, with a take-off distance available of over 1,090 yards, being used by flying schools, air-taxi companies and private owner-flyers, using both fixed-wing aircraft and helicopters.

The South East Air Support Unit (previously the Sussex Police Air Operations Unit), which operates from Shoreham airport, was equipped in February 2000 with a McDonnel-Douglas MD 902 Explorer (G-SUSX). The unit, which is headed by the police, is supported by civilian pilots, paramedics and ground support staff,

Piper PA-28-181 Cherokee Archer G-LACD with Lancing College on 28 August 2010. (Adam Tinworth)

Robinson R.44 G-HHOG of FAST Helicopters Ltd on 30 July 2010. (Nigel Hodgson)

Panavia Tornado XX947 – the third prototype aircraft, and the first of the type to fly with dual controls – parked at the Transair Pilot Supplies building on 30 July 2010. (Nigel Hodgson)

and a crew of three fly in the helicopter on any 'call', and can reach any part of Sussex (around 1,500 square miles) within twenty minutes.

On 2 April 2001, both engines of twin-engined Piper PA-34-220T (G-OMAR) failed on the aircraft's approach to land at Shoreham, and, looking for a suitable place to land, the pilot struck the roof of a house adjacent to the railway line on the south-west side of the bridge opposite St Peter's Catholic church. The aircraft was on a return flight from Sheffield when, as the pilot began a shallow left turn for runway 21, he informed ATC that he was having a problem with the left engine. As he was cleared for a wide left-hand circuit, the engine failed completely. During an attempt to restart it, the right engine also failed, and he was told to land on grass runway 25, the nearest to him. By this time, however, the aircraft had descended to about 900 feet, with both propellers windmilling. Further engine restart attempts were made, but with the aircraft now at 400 feet and pointing directly at the airfield, the pilot realised that he would be unable to glide to the runway, and he began looking for a suitable place to land. Noticing a narrow strip of grass between a railway line and the end of several rows of houses, the pilot aimed for this area and lowered the landing gear. As he approached the grass area the pilot flared the aircraft, but the left wing struck the roof of a house, and the right wing

Beagle B.206 Bassett G-ARRM outside the Northbrook College hangar on 30 July 2010. (Nigel Hodgson)

Enstrom 480 G-TRUD undergoing maintenance with FAST Helicopters on 30 July 2010. (Nigel Hodgson)

and tailplane struck an adjacent tree. The roof collapsed, absorbing much of the aircraft's forward speed, and the aircraft yawed left and slid into the rear garden of the house largely intact. Fire 1 (the first response vehicle) and Fire 2 (the fire pump) attended immediately from the airport fire station. The pilot suffered head injuries but was able to exit the aircraft unassisted. He later returned to the cockpit to switch off the aircraft electrical systems.

The Real Flying Company was formed at Shoreham airport in 2002 by two professional pilots and their wives – Neil and Lisa Westwood and Mike and Kathy Chapman – with the aim of rekindling a bygone era of flying. With a team of dedicated and highly skilled instructors, pilots and ground crew, and their niche fleet of a 1947 Stampe SV4C (G-AYCK), two 1952 De Havilland Chipmunks (G-BZGA/WK 585), and G-BXGX/WK 586), a 1953 L18 Piper Super Cub (G-BLMR) and a Piper PA-28-161 Warrior III (G-OPUK), they offer clients the chance not only to experience a piece of aviation history but also to introduce them to a corner of aviation which is the envy of many modern pilots.

Shoreham airport was advertised as being for sale by the local authority in *Flight International Magazine* of 24 January 2005. The advert stated that the airport

Cessna 525 OO-CEJ awaiting passengers on 30 July 2010. (Nigel Hodgson)

produced a tenanted income of around £840,000, an insufficient amount and an indication that the airport was probably being run at a loss.

Dorothy Saul-Pooley, who ran courses to train flying instructors and examiners for Sky Leisure in 1999–2000, started her own company, Pooley's Flying Instructor School (probably the only dedicated instructor training school run by a woman in the UK), in March 2005, offering training to candidates who held a CPL or ATPL in basic instruction, instrument, multi-engine, aerobatics, night and flight instruction. Having flown over eighty types of aircraft herself, and with around 9,500 flying hours (over 8,000 of these as an instructor), she has also conducted around 500 instructor and examiner tests, and has had around twenty flying manuals published. In March 2014, she was invested as Master of the Honourable Company of Air Pilots.

In honour of one of the pioneers of aviation at Shoreham, an 835 Dennis Trident of Metro Line 49 that was given the name *Cecil Pashley* upon its delivery to the company, in 2000, continued to bear the same name when the vehicle (W835NNJ) was re-liveried in 2005.

A North American B-25 Mitchell on 16 August 2007. (Neil Hilton)

A view of Shoreham airport across the runway on 29 April 2005. (Al Peterson)

A Miles M.38 Messenger 2A, G-AIEK/RG333, on 21 August 2010. (Steven Whitehead)

A Spitfire banks round over the airfield at the Shoreham air display in 2008. (Nick Denbow)

The tragic Hurricane crash at Shoreham Airshow on 15 September 2007. (Alan (Fred) Pipes)

The prototype Beagle B.206X created nostalgic moments when she returned home in May. The aircraft had not fared at all well in the intervening years; she was missing both engines and only one propeller had survived. Former Rolls-Royce Engineer Brian Newby (who worked closely with Beagle Aircraft during the B.206 development programme) sourced two compatible replacement engines, and over a two-year period, while the aircraft was in the care of a small band of skilled volunteers working on her preservation and restoration, Brian got both engines to running condition.

On the taxiway on 11 October 2008. (Les Chatfield)

SkySouth's Piper PA-31 Navajo Chieftain G-STHA on 7 June 2011. (Rob Finch)

A beautiful vintage De Havilland Rapide, G-AGTM, holds short of Shoreham's grass runway 25 while a Cessna 150 lands with Lancing College in the background on 7 August 2011. (Rob Finch)

Avro Lancaster PA-474, *The Phantom of the Ruhr*, part of the BBMF, at Shoreham during the 2011 airshow. (Steven Whitehead)

Miles M.38 Messenger RG333 and a Dakota DC-3 (N147DC/210084/L4-D) on 19 August 2011. (Clive Barker)

Shoreham airport's 1930s tower and terminal building on 21 June 2011. (Clive Barker)

Top: A flat pack of nine reds on 16 July 2011. (Tim Aldworth)

Left: 212 Squadron at the ready at the Shoreham Airshow in 2009. (Les Chatfield)

Above: Christian Moullec with his microlight and formation of geese at the 2008 airshow. (Debbie Marten)

CHAPTER 9

2006–2014
All Change

Due to mounting debts, Shoreham airport was sold by Brighton & Hove City Council and Worthing Borough Council to the Erinaceous Group PLC in July 2006 for £8.6 million. The new owners had already indicated that they anticipated an increase in flights to European destinations and short-hop flights to places like Edinburgh, but after spending around four months discussing its plans with the Civil Aviation Authority and local councils, they played down the speculation of any large-scale expansion. They did, however, attract the German plane manufacturer Piper to Shoreham, where it would establish its UK base. This would include sales and demonstration aircraft and a spare parts service. It also proposed to restore the listed terminal building as well as creating a new aviation square (two new three-storey mixed-use buildings flanking the terminal building) and an operations centre.

Skysouth was founded at Shoreham in 2006. They set up their office in the reception area of the terminal building, and from Wednesday 1 August began a twice-daily service to Paris (Pontoise) using Piper Navajo aircraft, with flights departing Shoreham at 0800 hours and 1530 hours, and departing Pontoise at 1040 hours and 1810 hours, adding to their service to Le Touquet. The company began scheduled flights to Deauville on 11 January 2008 with their twin-engined, eight-seat Piper PA-31-350 Navajo Chieftain (G-OETV) Commuter aircraft, but ceased trading in February 2009 after economic conditions made their operations no longer financially viable.

Plans to radically overhaul and modernise the infrastructure of the airport in order to transform it into a community and aviation business hub, creating up to 200 new jobs, were submitted to the Adur District Council by the Erinaceous Group PLC on 14 May 2007. The overhaul aimed to reflect the regeneration of the town of Shoreham, and the proposals included a restoration of the airport's famous 1930s art deco terminal building, and the arrival and departure functions

Shoreham airport Control Car No.1 (V352 KKL), a 1999 Land Rover, on 25 July 2012. (Clive Barker)

A 1988 Mercedes-Benz avgas tanker on 31 August 2012. (Clive Barker)

A BAC Jet Provost T-5 against the backdrop of the funfair in 2012. (Clive Barker)

(which at the time took place in another building), as well as the construction of several new buildings, including a new hangar, a new fire station and control tower, and offices which would be rented out to local businesses. In what was believed to be a first for UK airports, the designs also included on-site apartments, in a design comparable to houses at the nearby Brighton Marina.

The pre-war GV II VR2 hangar at the airport was given Grade II status (ID No. 503030) on 20 August 2007. It was designated because it was a relatively uncommon hangar design that had a distinctive double-span form and roof profile, which, although not innovative or technologically unusual for its date, was representative of contemporary interwar trends in hangar design. In addition, despite some rebuilding and modification following damage sustained in the Second World War, the essential structure was original. The hangar also bore witness to the phenomenal growth of civil aviation during the 1930s, a pioneering and audacious episode of considerable historic interest, which was otherwise recognised in very few designated sites.

A Canadian Vickers Canso A amphibian (a PBY-5A Catalina built under licence), *Miss Pick Up* (G-PBYA), on 31 August 2012. (Clive Barker)

Robinson R.22 Beta G-BTBA outside the workshops of FAST Helicopters Ltd, with SX-HVR. (Clive Barker)

Legendary flying instructor Toon Ghose, who had been the CFI for Cecil Pashley and the Southern Aero Club and later ran his own business, Toon Ghose Aviation, decided to hang up his flying helmet after more than 14,000 hours' flying, 9,000 of which were completed in circuits. Those who had flown with Ghose reflected on what a good pilot and instructor he was.

Tragedy struck at the 2007 RAFA Air Display on 15 September, when a Second World War Hawker Hurricane (G-HURR) crashed near Lancing College. The pilot, Brian Brown, who flew planes in the James Bond film *Tomorrow Never Dies*, was killed instantly.

The £1.5-million aircraft was taking part in a mock battle with the BBMF and was following another Hurricane in a tail chase. Both aircraft flew past the spectators along the display line at a height of approximately 200 feet before tracking to the north-west and climbing. The leading Hurricane rolled left, and Brian rolled his aircraft right. However, it reached the inverted position at around 700 feet, with insufficient nose-up pitch attitude, and the roll stopped, the nose dropped, and the aircraft entered a steep dive and impacted the ground. The air show was delayed for about thirty minutes, but organisers announced over the tannoy system that the pilot would have wanted them to carry on. Spitfires carried out a flypast in the 'man missing in action' formation, and despite the horrific accident, the air show raised in excess of £150,000 for the RAFA, which was a record achievement.

Welcome to Shoreham (Brighton City) Airport, 1 December 2012. (Clive Barker)

The prop of a Hawker Hurricane Mk2b (G-HHII – XP-L) screwing into the damp air; it was flown by the owner, Peter Teichman, at the RAFA Battle of Britain Airshow at Shoreham on 2 September 2012. (Martin Dighton)

CH9-8 Nord 1002 Pingouin II G-ETME in a simulated airfield attack at the Shoreham Airshow on 2 September 2012. (Martin Dighton)

With passenger numbers down by 37 per cent, and air traffic movements down by 31 per cent on the previous year, the Erinaceous Group PLC went into administration on Monday 14 April with debts of £250 million, bringing an end to a corporate tale of rapid expansion and equally rapid decline. The airport was closed, and KPMG (Klynveld Peat Marwick Goerdeler) administrators were appointed. Trading on the stock exchange was suspended, and all flights were grounded amid fears that their insurance may no longer be valid. Albemarle Shoreham Airport Ltd, which already owned the commercial buildings at Shoreham, bought the Erinaceous Group's interest the following day, bringing the airport back under one controlling company. The requirement made of Albemarle was to ensure that the airport remained operational for a minimum of thirty-five years, and to invest a minimum of £4 million in redeveloping and refurbishing the premises as contained in the airport lease. The regeneration plans for the airport by the company were said to be in accordance with the vision held by the joint-owning councils, when the airport was originally sold in 2006. The airport reopened for business immediately after legal negotiations took place, and by mid-afternoon, Skysouth operated the first scheduled flights to Cannes and Deauville.

Reims F172H Skyhawk G-SACD on 31 August 2012. (Clive Barker)

Reims F172H Skyhawk G-SACD on 31 August 2012. (Clive Barker)

Flying Time Aviation took over the Flying Hut in the main terminal building, and later took over what was Airbase flying club in the old customs hall, offering pilot training in one of the most modern fleets of training aircraft in the world. The company also offered Flight Training Adelaide (FTA) simulators, and modular courses, such as airline transport pilot licence theory (ATPL), private pilot licence (PPL), multi engine rating (MEP), multi engine commercial pilot licence (CPL), multi engine instrument rating (MEIR), and night rating (NR) were also available.

The 2008 air show (30–31 August) was started by Christian Moullec, who wowed the crowds with a truly unique display with his microlight and cranes (he usually uses geese) that fly with him. Raised from chicks, Moullec slowly taught them to follow him on the ground then fly alongside him in formation while he pilots the microlight. The air show also featured a special tribute to pilot Brian Brown, who had been killed during a display in a Hawker Hurricane at the previous year's show, and a memorial, erected just outside the main terminal building, was unveiled.

The hangars and buildings behind the terminal in May 2012. (Clare Rogers)

Curtiss P-40M Warhawk G-KITT rolls to take off for a display at the Shoreham Airshow on 1 September 2013. (Martin Dighton)

BAC Jet Provost T-5 XW324 departing for a display at the Eastbourne Air Show on 16 August 2013. (John Walton)

True to form, the weather deteriorated during the afternoon, leading to a few of the participants cancelling their displays.

Sixteen-year-old Rowan Lawson took advantage of the mild weather at the airport on Tuesday 14 October to join the growing list of young pilots around the country who completed their first solo flights on their sixteenth birthdays, but Rowan, having soloed fixed wing in Bulldog (G-CBGX) in the morning, took it one step further in the afternoon by taking to the sky alone in an Enstrom F28A helicopter (G-BBPO).

Shoreham airport was chosen to receive the first approved RNAV (aRea NAVigation) global navigation satellite system (GNSS) non-precision approach for general aviation in the UK by the UK Civil Aviation Authority (CAA). The system, which uses global positioning system (GPS), was introduced on 20 November 2008. The approach was made available to aircraft and crew meeting the necessary requirements from 20 November for both 02 and 20 runways. The requirements for pilots and aircraft were that:

Pilots flying the approach must have a current Instrument Rating (IR) or an Instrument Meteorological Conditions Rating (IMCR). The aircraft navigation system installation, based upon GNSS receiver equipment qualified to (E)TSO-C129a (certain classes only) or (E)TSO-C145 or (E)TSO-C146, had to be approved for the purpose.

A simulated engine fire on a Boeing B-17G Flying Fortress, *Sally B* (G-BEDF), displaying at the Shoreham Airshow on 31 August 2013. (Martin Dighton)

The first commercially registered Blackhawk B200, a nine-seat executive aircraft owned by Air Charter, was completed by MCA Aviation Ltd on 19 December 2008. The aircraft was a major modification to the Beechcraft King Air B200, making it faster, with a longer range, being more fuel-efficient, and having a shorter take-off and landing capacity.

Aero Alliance was formed in early 2009, with Captain Stuart Rawlinson as the senior pilot, to promote and develop charter flight operations and other aviation services to meet the demands of groups of up to seven people from Shoreham and other airports in the South East. Their niche was that, unlike a scheduled flight operator, which is limited to a few destinations, the charter flight was able to fly to any destination with a runway long enough for the aircraft to legally operate.

John Haffenden, who had been the airport general manager since 1993, resigned on 14 October 2009 after a dispute with the managing owners, Albemarle (Shoreham Airport) Ltd.

Haffenden had lobbied and worked with the CAA, and was instrumental in expediting the construction of taxiway 'K', and the installation of the GPS approach.

Douglas C-47 N147DC at Shoreham Airshow on 31 August 2013. (Steven Whitehead)

Fairey Swordfish Mk1 LS326 at Shoreham Airshow on 31 August 2013. (Steven Whitehead)

De Havilland Tiger Moths at the 2013 Shoreham Airshow. (Tim Harland)

Fairey Swordfish and Jet Provost at the 2013 Shoreham Airshow. (Tim Harland)

North American B-25 Mitchell at the 2013 Shoreham Airshow. (Tim Harland)

The old Skysouth offices in the terminal building were taken over by Jonathan Pointer, who set up a gift shop and also sold jams, pickles, curds, mustard and chutneys sourced from top-quality producers. A veritable Aladdin's cave, plans were in hand to include quality souvenir items specific to the airport. The shop was closed in February 2010.

The Bar & Restaurant in Terminal 2 reopened as Airside 2 Bar & Diner in October 2009 with new caterers, Convex Leisure. This came only a month after the company had refurbished Café Express, which overlooks the runway from the art deco main terminal, where The Beagle Suite conference room was also opened on the first floor.

In February 2010, Convex Leisure announced its plans to revamp Wingfield House (named after George Wingfield, who founded the airport in 1909) with a new look aimed at encouraging the younger generation of pilots, aviation enthusiasts and members of the general public to visit.

The 2010 air show marked the 70th anniversary of the Battle of Britain, as well as its own 100th anniversary, and was to host a number of displays to celebrate this important milestone. However, most of the display aircraft were unable to attend due to low cloud and adverse weather conditions on both days, claimed to

Douglas C-47 2100884 at the 2013 Shoreham Airshow. (Tim Harland)

have been the worst for twenty-one years. One display that did go ahead nearly ended in tragedy, when on 22 August, pilot Mike Newman, who was performing for the Swift Aerobatic Display Team, lost control of his high-performance Swift S-1 glider only minutes after it was released from its towline, and fell to the runway in front of around 15,000 onlookers. Despite the cockpit being smashed to pieces on impact, the former racing driver managed to crawl out of the wreckage. As he was taken away on a stretcher, doctors at the scene revealed that he had sustained a back injury.

Transair (Flight Equipment) opened their new flagship aviation showroom at the airport in November. The newly revamped facility had been enlarged to a total floor area of 2,500 feet^2. Outside the shop is the gate guard – the third prototype of the Tornado (XX947), which took its maiden flight from BAE Warton on 5 August 1975, and was primarily used for flight-testing in the development of the Tornado, flying for a total of 1,830 hours.

Two light aircraft collided over Shoreham on 4 July 2011, resulting in one fatality. A DA40 Diamond Star (G-CEZR) hit a Vans RV-6A (G-RVGC) at right angles, removing its fin and rudder and the tip of the left tailplane, rendering the RV6 uncontrollable. It crashed in an open area at the Adur recreation ground,

A Redhill Charters Piper PA-31-350 Navajo Chieftain, G-OJIL, on the ramp at Shoreham airport on 13 August 2013. (Trevor Hall)

killing the pilot; debris was found as far away as Shoreham beach. The Diamond Star lost its propeller and a badly holed wing leading edge, but the pilot managed to land safely on the non-active runway 25.

On 29 September, a seventy-five-year-old pilot was lucky to walk away with just minor cuts after his aircraft, a Taylorcraft BC.12D Twosome (G-BSDA), somersaulted on landing, and ended up on its roof at the end of the runway. The flight from Rowhook, West Sussex, had been uneventful, and the pilot was expecting an approach to runway 20, but was instead directed to land on runway 13. However, he reported that he 'mentally scrambled' the runway numbers and positioned for an approach to runway 31. He touched down smoothly at an airspeed of 55 mph, after which he observed the remaining landing distance available reducing rapidly (the runway is 446 yards long). He applied heavy braking, and the aircraft flipped over.

The Defence Review in early November had a profound effect on the Royal Air Force, and a number of aircraft types were retired, with several squadrons hanging up their colours awaiting their next incarnation. One of them was 14 Squadron, which was formed at Shoreham in 1915 and celebrated its association with the airfield with a flypast of a Tornado GR4 on 29 March as a final farewell before its disbandment on 1 June 2011.

Piper PA-38-112 Tomahawk G-BGRX outside its hangar on 14 December 2013. (Trevor Hall)

The BREAST (Brooklands Recovery Engineering and Salvage Team) boys arrived early in the morning of 10 December to transport the Beagle B.206X prototype (G-ARRM) to the FAST museum at Farnborough for restoration. Marking the end of its long association with the airport, her wings were removed and, using lifting equipment loaned by Langley Vale of Epsom, she was loaded onto a transporter.

In 2012, the Fly-in Bar & Restaurant in the main terminal building was rebranded as the Hummingbird Café (named after Harold Piffard's self-built *Hummingbird* pusher biplane, which made its debut in 1910) by the local bakery firm Truffles, and, although redecoration was carried out, the art deco features were retained, the huge windows overlooking the airfield being the prime examples.

Lancing College purchased the Sussex Pad Hotel, which is located on the edge of the school's estate in Old Shoreham Road, after it had been on the market for around eighteen months without attracting any serious interest from buyers. The decision to sell was made by its owners, Sue Pack and her husband Wally, because of the difficult economic conditions, and because of Wally's health.

Adur District Council and Worthing Borough Council produced a strategic flood risk assessment (SFRA) update in January 2012. As a functional floodplain

The Breitling Wingwalkers (AeroSuperBatics Ltd) on 16 August 2013. Founded in 1989 by Vic Norman, a veteran aerobatics pilot, they operate four Boeing-Stearman Model 75 biplanes. The team's shows consist of aerobatic manoeuvres while female athletes, attached to a post above the wings, engage in acrobatics. (John Walton)

(the airport was designated Flood Zone 3b), development was ruled out until the Tidal Walls Scheme for the Adur had been completed, and measures such as surface water run-off and the use of sustainable drainage systems had to be included in any future development plans in that area to help reduce the flood risk and protect properties and businesses on both the east and west banks of the river.

New development for aviation-related B1 (Business), B2 (General Industrial) and B8 (Storage and Distribution) uses, as well as other appropriate ancillary employment-generating uses, continued to be supported on the existing developed area located at the southern end of the airport.

A meeting was held in 2013, and a notam was issued following concerns that had been raised by Southern Trains and National Rail about the low height at which aircraft were crossing the railway line just south of the runway 02 threshold. After this safety issue had come to the attention of the SRG (safety regulation group) at the CAA, and the airport's ATC and management alike, advice was given to pilots (based as well as visiting ones) about using the PAPIs (precision approach path indicators) to ensure that enough clearance is obtained, and that three whites are used to counter any downdraught or 'low and slow' scenario. Two reds and two whites are for a 3.5° glideslope on this runway, and light aircraft are more than capable of using a much steeper approach than that used by large commercial air transport. A steeper glideslope would also safeguard against any possible engine failure on approach, and help an aircraft to reach the safety of the airfield boundary, should the worst ever happen. Incidents where the undercarriage of an approaching aircraft was as close as 10 feet to a passing train had been recorded.

Above and below: Dassault MD-312 Flamants F-AZGE/12XA and F-AZKT/318KT resting at Shoreham between shows at Eastbourne with a Southern Railway Class 313 three-car EMU heading west along the South Coast on 16 August 2013. (John Walton)

The terminal building on 16 August 2013. (John Walton)

Brighton City Airways (BCA) launched a twice-daily scheduled service to France following the launch of the new airline on 6 March. Its Czech-built LET L-410 Turbolet commuter aircraft (OK-ASA) carried a maximum of nineteen passengers for the one-hour flight to Pontoise, Paris, and BCA was advised by the French authorities that there would be a short delay of a couple of weeks before a customs and immigration port of entry was in place at Paris Pontoise. In the meantime, the aircraft would land at Rouen or Le Touquet airports en-route to Pontoise, although the authorities very rarely boarded to check passports. Having two take-offs and climbs instead of one, extra airport feed, longer flight times and additional maintenance costs, BCA announced that the service would be suspended from 7 May, and would be exploring new routes. Effective from that date, there have been no further scheduled services operating out of the airport.

Speculation was rife in July when Albemarle (Shoreham Airport) Ltd looked to take over the freehold of the airport from Brighton & Hove City Council. With further cuts being made to town halls by the Government, and austerity biting, the council's roles had changed dramatically, and a review was made of the viability of maintaining the airport with a reduced budget; they were considering transferring their ⅔ ownership of the freehold. Worthing Borough Council was also approached as owner of the remaining ⅓ of the freehold to try to strike a deal. Finally, at a press conference on Thursday 29 November, it was announced that Shoreham airport would be rebranded as Brighton (Shoreham) airport.

The Sussex coast was badly hit by a tidal surge in December, which flooded roads, completely closing the A259, and put the railway line out of action. The airfield was closed after being flooded when the River Adur burst its banks. Temporary repairs were made over the following twenty-four hours by the Environment Agency, and, although the airport was able to reopen, many of the businesses affected on the site took longer to get back to normal. The airport management worked closely with the Adur, Worthing and Brighton & Hove councils, and other major stakeholders in Shoreham, including Shoreham Port, Ricardo PLC (engineering providers for transportation, defence and clean energy industries) and Northbrook College, to secure the funding for new tidal walls for the River Adur.

The year 2014 is a significant one for the whole of Europe, with two major events: seventy years ago, the Allies landed in Europe during Operation Overload, or D-Day, on 6 June 1944. Shoreham harbour was one of the bases for the Allied build-up, and this theme will feature prominently during the show in August, which will be the twenty-fifth RAFA Shoreham Airshow, and will see the first appearance of the Irish Historic Flight with two De Havilland Types; a DH-84 Dragon 'Iolar', and two De Havilland Canada Chipmunks, which have been restored into

colours of the Irish Air Corps. The second event of the year, which will also be commemorated at the air show, is the 100th anniversary of the start of the First World War on 28 July 1914. The Great War Display Team will be recreating the hectic skies over the First World War battlefield with their wonderful replicas, which include a trio of Royal Aircraft Factory (RAF) SE5as, a Sopwith Triplane, a pair of Fokker Dr1 triplanes, two Junkers CL1s, and Matthew Boddington's RAF BE2c.

A Cessna 501 Citation (N452TS) that departed Shoreham mid-morning on 12 January crashed in poor visibility near Trier, Germany. The privately owned aircraft carrying four passengers was on the approach to land at Trier-Föhren airport when it struck an electricity pylon. The pilot lost control, and the aircraft crashed at a landfill site close-by, killing the four occupants.

Plans were submitted by Albemarle (Shoreham Airport) Ltd in early January for a multimillion-pound development at the airport, with a focus on the buildings, which are badly cracked; the domed roof of the terminal foyer has been removed, and water damage is spreading across the site.

Shoreham airport is still at the forefront of general aviation in this country. Its Grade II listed terminal building is still in everyday use by business, training and pleasure fliers alike, including many visitors from Europe. The visitor centre, which offers airport guided tours, features exhibits on the airport's aviation history in the area, and has an archive library of related historic materials. The airport also houses Northbrook College's engineering department, a Centre of Vocational Excellence in Aerospace and Aviation, and a number of aerospace and commercial aviation businesses have offices and workshops both in the site and along the perimeter road. A number of operators provide sightseeing and pleasure flights in vintage aeroplanes, and the airport is mainly used by privately owned light aircraft for business and pleasure, and for aircraft and helicopter sales. It remains under the ownership of Albemarle (Shoreham Airport) Limited.

Opposite above: Piper J3C-90 Cub G-OCUB on 6 October 2013. (Clive Barker)

Opposite below: Shoreham airport on Remembrance Sunday, 2013.

CHAPTER 10

Shoreham Airport Rescue and Firefighting Service (SARFFS)

Airports are categorised (in simple terms) according to the size of aircraft operated, and the number of movements of aircraft of a particular size. Shoreham airport today is a Category 2 airfield, the highest being Category 10. For example, a small private landing strip could be classed a Category 1; London Gatwick, with just one runway, is a Category 9; and London Heathrow airport, with two runways catering for far more flights and passengers each day, is a Category 10.

Shoreham airport has provided a rescue and firefighting service on its site for over ninety years. From the early days of flying there was a need for fuel, transport equipment, and motor vehicles to tow, for rescue and firefighting, and many of the first developments took place at the time when the motor car was in its early years, just like the early flying machines. It wasn't until the 1920s–1930s that fire engines manufactured for airports really got moving, though these were just modifications of standard civilian motor vehicles from the time, such as Bedford, Pyrene, Ford, HCB-Angus and Leyland. The first known airfield fire engine (crash tender) was a Model T Ford, which was adapted to carry a number of handheld extinguishers, a small chemical foam tank and a hose reel. Foam compound was carried in cylinders and mixed with water from an onboard tank. Due to the flimsy construction of aircraft during the early years of flying, and the proneness to easily crashing, the first priority was always the rescue of passengers and crew.

The situation hadn't changed much by the outbreak of war in September 1939. The military had already taken over many of the privately run airfields throughout the country, and Shoreham was no exception. The means of battling an aircraft fire would have been handheld extinguishers, buckets of water, stirrup pumps, and a hose reel, which would be connected up to a water supply and run out to the ill-fated aircraft, this being done by anyone who had the nerve to try and get close to the blazing aircraft to extinguish the fire. With most of the aircraft of the time being of wood and canvas construction, tragedy was inevitable on occasion,

North American P-51D Mustang 413521. (Steven Whitehead)

Shorts Tucano T-1 ZF171-LZR. (Steven Whitehead)

and although just a small fuel tank was fitted, fire was always a concern and a priority.

Purpose-built crash tenders were introduced to the RAF in 1937, among them the Crossley Teardrop crash tender (so-called after the shape of its enclosed cab), which carried a 200-gallon water tank, and twin air-foam pumps, which were driven by the vehicle's engine. The Fordson Sussex 6 x 4 crash tender was delivered in the same year. This had a fully enclosed cab and flat platform body, and would carry three 30-gallon froth extinguishers, twelve 2-gallon foam extinguishers and various hand tools.

Due to the size of the airport and the types of aircraft operating at the time, the airfield had at least two crash tenders, a 1938 Crossley FWD 3-ton 4 x 4, and a Fordson/Weeton type WOT1 3-ton Monitor Type 6 x 4 (which are known to have been still in use in the late 1950s). These were supported by ambulances (on the Austin K2 chassis), a wrecker truck, and a rescue unit, but these may well have been ex-RAF vehicles put in to service. Locally built conversions of American Jeeps were seen at many airfields across the country, in use as rescue trucks, and it is

The Blades' Extra 300L, G-XXTR, in mid-display. (Steven Whitehead)

worth noting that for many years after the war, much of this equipment remained in service at many airfields around the country, including Shoreham airport.

Following the end of hostilities, when the airfield was returned to civil use, new fire appliances were being made solely for airfield crash/rescue work, and became more available, and Shoreham airport was not far behind any other airfield in keeping up to the standards that were expected of it. During the 1960s, second-hand fire tenders were purchased from the local authorities: a Land Rover 4 x 4 109 Forward Control L4P appliance, and an ex-Brighton Fire Brigade Dennis pump. In recent years, ex-military crash tenders have continued to serve at the airport. A 1983 ex-Exeter airport Reynold/Boughton RB44 HCB-Angus RIV (Rapid Intervention Vehicle) was used until it was replaced by a large Scammell Nubian/Carmichael 4 x 4 Mk 10 crash tender, which served as 'Fire 3' until recent years when it, too, was replaced by a Scania P420.

Today, the riding strength of the rescue and firefighting service is eight full-time personnel, headed by a senior airport fire officer, who man four appliances on two watches (red and blue watches) on a three-on, three-off roster during the operating hours of the airport:

Red Watch
Watch Commander Dave Bennett
Crew Commander Andrew Corke
Firefighter Darren Greene
Firefighter Gareth Preece

Blue Watch
Watch Commander Dave Greenwood
Crew Commander Darren Burley
Firefighter Peter Moore
Firefighter Stuart Purves

The current fleet consists of four vehicles:

Fire 1 - A Carmichael-supplied vehicle (T410KNT), which is based on a Chevrolet Cheyenne C-3500 HD chassis cab, and powered by a 6.6-litre V8 turbo diesel engine, with automatic transmission (panel change). It is the first response vehicle at the airport, and is equipped with a self-contained pump, which is able to produce foam at speed and deliver through a roof-mounted monitor, independent of the vehicle engine. The pumping unit is a self-contained Godiva 10/10 unit, driven by a Honda BF45A (modified) engine – a single-stage, centrifugal pump manufactured by Godiva Ltd, with an output of 1,000 litres at 10 bar. Additional items of equipment carried by this appliance include 1 x standpipe key and bar, 4 x 45-mm (Dutch rolled) and 1 x 70-mm delivery hose, one Akron Turbo Jet Branch, Honda EB.3000X generator with tripods and floodlights with 50-m extension reel, 3 x section ladder and ceiling hook (roof mounted), loud hailer, asbestos blanket, 15-m and 30-m G-P line, sledgehammer, bolt croppers, crowbar, various axes and aircraft-type (non-wedging) axes, general-purpose handsaw, a Dewalt 24-volt battery saw, small toolbox, salvage sheets, 2 x blocks (step type), suction wrenches, 2 x lifejackets, first aid equipment and a stretcher.

Fire 2 - Another Carmichael-supplied vehicle (Q589VWP) and is powered by a 3.5-litre V8 engine. All three axles are driven, giving the vehicle good off-road capabilities, and its use is that of a fast-response/primary knockdown appliance. Fitted with a Godiva UFPX656/8 fire pump, the vehicle carries 900 litres of pre-mixed 6 per cent FFFP. Two sidelines are available, each fitted with one 30-m x 38-mm diameter length of hose flaked in the two side lockers and terminating in an aspirating Firechief Foam branch pipe. Once the vehicle has deployed its 900 litres of foam pre-mix, its job is done, as far as a pumping unit is concerned. The appliance also carries bolt croppers, crowbar, aircraft axe, a three-section ladder, a 15-m G-P line, first aid kit, fire blanket, a 5-kg CO_2 extinguisher, and a toolbox comprising all items of small/hand tools to comply with the standards required by the CAA for a CAT2 aerodrome.

Fire 3 – The Carmichael Viper. New to Shoreham airport in 2006, it is a 420-hp Scania P420 (VU06XYR) 4 x 4 right-hand-drive chassis, on which is mounted a specialist firefighting body with top hamper. It can accelerate from 0 to 50 mph in just twenty-three seconds, and carries 4,627 litres of water, with a foam tank capacity of 746 litres of class B FFFP foam compound for firefighting. Fire 3 also has an integral 220-litre training foam tank in its design that allows real foam production training to take place without the environmental issues. The appliance is fitted with a Hale 4010 WTA centrifugal two-stage firefighting pump; the first low-pressure high-volume stage supplies both delivery outlets and monitor, the second high-pressure low-volume stage can supply both water and water/foam combination, though non aspirated. The hose reel has 3 x 19 m of 19-mm bore hose, terminating in an 'Akron turbojet' branch mounted in the n/s rear locker. An Akron 3367 roof-mounted monitor is controlled by an in-cab control panel joystick, and delivers either 2,526 litres per minute in high-flow mode or 1,160 litres in low output, selected via an output rate control.

The foam system is complemented by two demountable Monnex dry powder units with a capacity of 50 kg each, located on both front lockers, and delivering media via their own discharge hoses. The nearside front locker contains hydraulic rescue equipment manufactured by Holmatro. The rescue equipment comprises a combination cutting and spreading/clamping tool, hydraulic pump powered by a two-stroke petrol engine, a hydraulic foot/hand pump, spreader ram complete with extension tubes, a chain set and pedal/restricted space cutting tool, and 15 m of hose. They also carry, in this locker, stability blocks and wedges, a Tirfor winch with cable, crowbar, and an aircraft axe.

Fire 4 – A Carmichael Commando Range Rover (B862SEC) 6 x 6 driven by a 3.9-litre V8 petrol injection engine. Like Fire 2, all three axles are driven, giving the vehicle good off-road capabilities. It is fitted with a Godiva UFPX 656/8 fire pump. The vehicle carries 900 litres of pre-mixed 6 per cent FFFP. Two sidelines are available, each fitted with one 30-m x 38-mm diameter length of hose, flaked into the side lockers and terminating in an aspirating Angus Foamaster B225 branch pipe. Once the vehicle has deployed its 900 litres of foam, its job is done as far as a pumping unit is concerned. The appliance also carries bolt croppers, ceiling hook, crowbar, aircraft axe, three-section ladder, a 15-m G-P line, first aid kit, fire blanket, two 5-kg CO_2 and two 9-kg Monnex DP extinguishers and a toolbox comprising all items of small/hand tools to comply with the standards required by the CAA for a CAT2 operation.

Shoreham airport's aircraft fuelling service is operated as a department of the RFFS. There are three large mobile fuel bowsers for delivering both Avgas and jet fuel to aircraft, including a service (accompanied by fire appliances) for fast delivery of fuel to police and coastguard emergency helicopters without disengaging their engines. Fuel technicians are attached to the firefighting watches and work the same shift pattern. There are two static Avgas fuel pumps supplied via three underground tanks with a capacity of some 50,000 litres, and two mobile Avgas bowsers. Jet fuel is supplied from another mobile bowser, which holds some 6,000 litres, or directly from a jet installation. The jet installation holds approximately 50,000 litres.

The RFFS also has a tractor with front-loader and rear flail or topper, a Hayter sit-on mower, a Honda quad-bike with a rotary topper and flail cutter, as well as petrol strimmers for grass cutting and controlling weeds along the taxiways and runways, keeping the operational lighting and edges clear and unobstructed.

Under the wire goes the Tiger Club Turbulent! (Steven Whitehead)

The Real Flying Company founders, Neil and Lisa Westwood, with Mike and Kathy Chapman in front of their 1952 De Havilland Chipmunk (WK585). (Ella Bartczak)

Dorothy Saul-Pooley was invested as Master of the Honourable Company of Air Pilots in March 2014. (Gerald Sharp Photography)

Aerodrome safety is, of course, paramount to its successful operation. At Shoreham, the RFFS support the management in ensuring its safe and efficient operation. At the start of each day, a full visual inspection of all areas is carried out, and the lighting systems on the surfaced runways and taxiways, the illuminated windsock and helicopter pad, the aircraft parking areas, fences, gates, and all border markers are checked, and all before the airport opens at 0900 hours. Evening lighting and surface inspections are also made on the request of ATC, and the service is always on call should anything become damaged during the operational hours.

Photographs of Shoreham

Art deco clock in the terminal. (Clive Barker)

An Avro D prototype at Barrow. (Author's Collection)

Beagle 206 (G-ATHO) at Shoreham in 1966. (Nick Denbow)

Beagle B206 (G-ARXM). (Donald Gray)

Beagle B206 (G-ASOF). (Donald Gray)

Beagle B206 (G-ATHO). (Donald Gray)

A Bentley, seen outside Shoreham. (Donald Gray)

Henri Farman III biplane, seen here in Bournemouth in 1910. (Author's Collection)

The remains of one of the pillboxes by the towpath on the western bank of the River Adur. (Richard Narramore)

The remains of one of the pillboxes by the towpath on the western bank of the River Adur. (Richard Narramore)

The control tower, hangars and aircraft at Shoreham airport on 30 October 2010. (Richard Narramore)

The control tower, hangars and aircraft at Shoreham airport on 30 October 2010. (Richard Narramore)

Taxiing back after landing at Shoreham airport on 6 November 2010. (Richard Narramore)

The Old Shoreham Tollbridge over the River Adur. (Richard Narramore)

An aircraft taking off from the runway at Shoreham airport. (Richard Narramore)

The perimeter road around Shoreham airport. (Richard Narramore)

The gun mount at the Old Fort, Shoreham. (Clive Barker)

The low bridge entrance to Shoreham airport – Northside. (Clive Barker)

The low bridge entrance to Shoreham airport – Southside. (Clive Barker)

The Old Adur Bridge, Shoreham. (Clive Barker)

The Old Shoreham Tollbridge over the River Adur. Lancing College Chapel is in the distance. (Richard Narramore)

Shoreham Fort. (Richard Narramore)

A 1994 Carmichael Chevrolet rescue tender of the Shoreham airport Rescue and Fire Fighting Service in 2011. (Clive Barker)

A 2008 MAN avgas tanker (DK58 JGZ) and a 2006 Scania P420 foam fire tender (YU06 XYR). (Clive Barker)

A 1994 Leyland DAF avgas tanker (M752 YWB) in 2011. (Clive Barker)

Shoreham airport Rescue & Fire Fighting Service vehicles. (Clive Barker)

A 1989 Carmichael Range Rover of Shoreham airport Fire and Rescue. (Clive Barker)

Above: The ground floor inside the art deco terminal in 2012. (Chris Sampson)

Left: Inside the art deco terminal in 2012. (Chris Sampson)

Right: Inside the art deco terminal in 2012. (Chris Sampson)

Below: Inside the art deco terminal in 2012. (Chris Sampson)

Left: The front of the art deco terminal in 2012. (Chris Sampson)

Below: The art deco terminal in 2012. (Chris Sampson)

The art deco terminal in 2012. (Chris Sampson)

The art deco terminal in 2012. (Chris Sampson)

Above left: Inside the art deco terminal in 2012. (Chris Sampson)

Above right: A plaque commemorating the opening of the terminal on 13 June 1936 hangs in the terminal building. (Chris Sampson)

The Hummingbird real ale bar and diner in the art deco terminal at Shoreham airport, on 16 November 2012. (Trevor Hall)

Tornado PO3, XX947, was the third Tornado prototype, and is pictured outside the Transair Pilot Shop at Shoreham airport on 16 November 2012. (Trevor Hall)

The station at Shoreham-by-Sea from Platform 2 on 30 April 2012. (Trevor Hall)

A Mercedes-Benz avgas tanker on 6 October 2013. (Clive Barker)

A 2008 MAN avgas tanker and Fire 3, a 2006 Scania P420 foam fire tender, on 21 June 2011. (Clive Barker)

Shoreham main building in the 1960s. (Donald Grey)

The weather station enclosure in the centre of the airfield. (Adrian Taylor)

Shoreham airfield from the air. (Donald Grey)

A H900 helicopter of Sussex Police at Shoreham. (Al Peterson)

Toon Ghose at his home in
Henfield in April 2014.

Toon Ghose with his daughter
Katie, and granddaughter
Anila Harrop, at his home in
Henfield, April 2014.

Toon Ghose with his daughter
Katie at his home in Henfield,
April 2014.

Bibliography

Brooks, Robin J., *Sussex Airfields in the Second World War*, 1993.

Darren Burley, Crew Commander (Blue Watch), Shoreham Airport RFFS.

Dorothy Saul-Pooley.

Dundee Courier, August 1948.

Fighter Interception Unit ORB, the National Archives, Kew.

Flight Magazine, various.

Fortean Times, May 2006.

Katie Ghose.

Marie Llewellyn (www.golfmissinglinks.co.uk).

Martyn Blunden, Omega Aviation.

Pete Matten, ex-West Sussex Fire Brigade.

Safety Regulation Group, Safety Investigation & Data Department.

Shoreham Airport News.

The Air Accident Investigation Bureau.

The Argus, various.

The Aviation Safety Network.

The Real Flying Company.

The Shoreham Herald, various.

Webb, T. M. A. and D. L. Bird, *Shoreham Airport, Sussex* (1999).